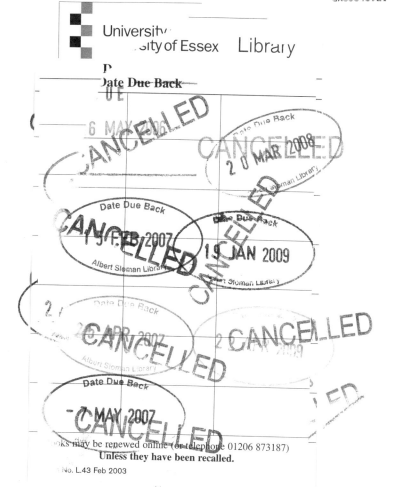

DOSTOEVSKY ON EVIL AND ATONEMENT

The Ontology of Personalism in His Major Fiction

DOSTOEVSKY ON
EVIL AND ATONEMENT

The Ontology of Personalism in His Major Fiction

Linda Kraeger

and

Joe Barnhart

The Edwin Mellen Press
Lewiston/Queenston/Lampeter

Library of Congress Cataloging-in-Publication Data

Kraeger, Linda.
  Dostoevsky on evil and atonement : the ontology of personalism in
his major fiction / Linda Kraeger and Joe Barnhart.
      p.   cm.
  Includes bibliographical references and index.
  ISBN 0-7734-9189-9
  1. Dostoyevsky, Fyodor, 1821-1881--Religion. 2. Dostoyevsky,
Fyodor, 1821-1881--Philosophy. 3. Evil in literature.
I. Barnhart, Joe E., 1931- . II. Title.
PG3328.Z7E95 1992
891.73'3--dc20

                                                              92-37926
                                                                  CIP

A CIP catalog record for this book
is available from the British Library.

The Edwin Mellen Press   The Edwin Mellen Press
        Box 450   Box 67
  Lewiston, New York   Queenston, Ontario
    USA 14092   CANADA, L0S 1L0

                  The Edwin Mellen Press, Ltd.
                    Lampeter, Dyfed, Wales
                  UNITED KINGDOM SA48 7DY

Printed in the United States of America

For
Duane Kraeger
devoted husband of twenty-six years,
whose enthusiasm and intellectual
curiosity never cease

and for

John H. Lavely
teacher par excellence

TABLE OF CONTENTS

Chapter   **Page Number**

TABLE OF CONTENTS

Chapter   **Page Number**

TABLE OF
CONTENTS

Chapter   **Page Number**

Acknowledgements

A number of individuals have helped us to complete this book. For their valuable comments on various parts of the manuscript, we wish to thank the following members of the University of North Texas faculty: Anthony Damico, Giles Mitchell, Max Oelschlaeger, L. Robert Stevens, and Eugene Wright.

Professor Richard Owsley, Regents Professor Stevens, and Dean Thomas Preston arranged for the noted Dostoevsky scholar Victor Terras of Brown University to come to the University of North Texas for a stirring Dostoevsky conference in 1987. No one who attempts to write on the great Russian novelist of the nineteenth century can afford to be ignorant of Professor Terras' contributions to Dostoevsky scholarship. Terras' performance at the Dostoevsky conference did much to inspire the writing of this book.

We owe a very special debt of gratitude to Kay Prewitt, who, working closely with us, typed and edited each chapter. Because of their remarkable ability to combine efficiency with cheerfulness, she and her colleagues, Betty Grise and Rachel Dowdy at the Data Entry Department, have helped make our work on each chapter a rewarding experience. Our warmest thanks to the three of them.

Lou Ann Bradley, Gary Sanders, and Jeffrey Levy of the UNT library staff have gone out of their way to assist us in our research over the years. Our thanks go to them and to many others of the library who in the busy back rooms serve daily our common cause of scholarship and the growth of knowledge.

Some writers have the misfortune of working in university departments cursed by jealousies, internecine hostilities, and sabotage. The UNT Department of Philosophy and Religion Studies is, by contrast, a spring of encouragement and support. We are grateful both to colleagues and to the department's secretary Kathryn Copeland for their many kindnesses and for the general tranquility conducive to research and writing.

Scholars from departments of literature, philosophy, and religion studies, as well as certain members of the American Academy of Religion contributed in one way or another to this volume. To them and to our students who have a passion for the nineteenth-century Russian novelists, we express our appreciation. Watson Mills of Mercer University has given encouragement and practical advice to a number of writers and researchers over the years. We wish to thank him for bringing us and The Edwin Mellen Press together.

Linda Kraeger wishes to express her thanks to administrators and faculty members at Grayson County Community College in Denison, Texas, who have supported her academic ventures. Not many educational institutions measure up to Grayson's capacity for fostering faculty development.

Acknowledgements

Mary Ann Barnhart has always encouraged her husband in his research and writing. This book offers no exception, despite Mary Ann's long hours at her own profession as a licensed counselor of Texas. Special thanks to her and to the Barnharts' son Rich and daughter Linda Jane.

Duane Kraeger began his contribution to this book twenty-eight years ago when he and Linda first met. From that time forward, he has shared with her a love of literature and learning for its own sake. Deepest thanks to him for his constant support.

Chapter I. The Laboratory of the Soul

Fyodor Mikhailovich Dostoevsky (1821-1881 C.E.) holds the distinction of having written four full-blown novels that continue to be ranked as classics. *Crime and Punishment*, *The Idiot*, *The Possessed*, and *The Brothers Karamazov* excel not only as works of art, but as bold philosophical and theological ventures. More a compendium of multiple plots than a gripping story, *A Raw Youth* fails as a literary achievement. The supreme combination of literary accomplishment and philosophical penetration, however, comes to conspicuous fruition in *The Brothers Karamazov*, Dostoevsky's crowning and final achievement. This novel overpowers everything else he wrote. In *The Idiot*, Dostoevsky had wished to create the Russian version of a Christ-like Don Quixote, Mr. Pickwick, or Jean

Valjean ("To His Niece" 141-4). Even though it is one of literature's greatest novels, Dostoevsky felt that it had not reached the height he had intended for it. In *The Brothers Karamazov*, his creative powers soar with a more robust and realistic portrayal of the "positively beautiful individual." His final work, Arther S. Trace aptly concludes, comes closest to expressing the whole of Dostoevsky's thought. "Compared to the fullness of *The Brothers Karamazov*, every other work of Dostoevsky's is fragmentary" (7).

Unmistakable and numerous footprints leading to the characters and themes in *The Brothers Karamazov* appear in the copious notes that Dostoevsky prepared for his large novels in particular. According to Dostoevsky scholar Robert L. Belknap, "Every novel or story he published contains elements that emerge again in *The Brothers Karamazov*" (*The Genesis* 45-6). In many ways, *A Raw Youth* along with hundreds of pages of notes for the novel served to prepare Dostoevsky for the Herculean work of writing the story of the Karamazovs.

The German philosopher Georg Hegel spoke of the World Spirit (*Weltgeist*) at war with itself. In *The Brothers Karamazov*, each of the brothers and minor characters wages an internal war. They live in a highly charged atmosphere of moral thunder reminiscent of Shakespeare's *King Lear* and generate philosophical lighting bolts found only in such masterpieces as *Hamlet* and the staggering plays of Aeschylus. Unlike *A Raw Youth*, *The Brothers Karamazov* explodes with life and passion while the plot drives forward with dramatic intensity. It remains as perhaps the world's greatest theological and philosophical novel for those with the intellectual courage to face the clash of two ideological fronts coming together to create a fierce emotional storm.

A year before he began the formal sketching of *The Brothers Karamazov*, Dostoevsky published both *The Dream of a Ridiculous Man* and *The Diary of a Writer*. The latter served in several ways as the proving ground of material to go into his final novel. *The Dream of a Ridiculous Man*, unlocking the mystery of his religious philosophy, makes it clear that Dostoevsky was a kind of postmillennialist, believing in the coming of the Kingdom of God to earth, to Mother Earth. Rejecting the secular socialist utopia, Dostoevsky set out to give concrete expression to his belief that precisely on the planet Earth love could overcome evil. Far from being an other-worldly mystic, Dostoevsky in a July-August, 1876, article titled "The Land and the Children" boldly asserted the doctrine of the sacramental earth. "There is something sacramental in the earth, in the soil" (*Diary* I). Like Rousseau and Thomas Jefferson, Dostoevsky believed that the human species would lose something fundamental of itself if it failed to cultivate its ties to nature, to the teeming animal and plant life dependent on the soil.

On May 16, 1878, when the formal outlining and sketching of the early chapters of *The Brothers Karamazov* had scarcely begun, Dostoevsky suffered a devastating shock, the death of his favorite child, three-year-old Alexei. It particularly distressed Dostoevsky that his son had perished from epilepsy, the illness that the father had passed on to the son. Until the child's death, Dostoevsky had not settled on a name for the youngest of the Karamazov brothers, who earlier in the rough drafts, even as late as April 1878, was called the "idiot." This term "idiot" has a special and even endearing meaning for Dostoevsky, who had titled an earlier novel *The Idiot*, the hero of which was Myshkin. Through Myshkin, the author had attempted to portray a good and beautiful soul in a world of conflict and evil.

The narrator of *The Brothers Karamazov* commits himself from the start to viewing the youngest of the Karamazov brothers, Alyosha (Alexei) Fyodorovich, as the story's hero. Dostoevsky in the very first sentence of the opening paragraph of his "From the Author" refers to Alexei Fyodorovich as "my hero." Belknap suggests that *Hamlet* is the longest of Shakespeare's plays because Shakespeare wished to create a rich identity for the namesake of his son Hamnet, who had died shortly before Shakespeare wrote the play (*The Genesis* 54). *The Brothers Karamazov* is Dostoevsky's longest work, perhaps in part because Dostoevsky found it difficult to cease making a life for Alexei (Goddard 332). At the end of the novel, Alexei Karamazov at the age of twenty delivers a moving affirmation of immortality. It is difficult not to believe that the words flow from a father who had recently lost his dearest.

Only after years of trial, error, and reformulation did Dostoevsky fully form the character in *The Brothers Karamazov* whom he named "Alexei." In *The Idiot*, Dostoevsky wished to portray the life of a good human being amid cruelty, perversity, and debauchery. Myshkin, the Christ-like figure of the novel, possesses a kind of naiveté that attracts people with its warmth and magnanimity. Alyosha (Alexei), representing a more vigorous mutation of Myshkin, maintains Myshkin's compassion and gentleness but brings to them a robustness and realism that the earlier experiment in human goodness lacked. Alyosha, entering the Karamazov's story as a youth scarcely in the bloom of early manhood, proves to be the great listener, the confidant to whom people feel free to reveal their thoughts, desires, and passions.

Alyosha so resembles the hero of *The Idiot* that the reader might easily confuse them and fail to grasp the change in Dostoevsky's own mind regarding the embodiment of goodness. If Myshkin represents Christianity's focus on the crucifixion, Alyosha represents the resurrection. Alyosha's last words in the novel deal with resurrection, and several factors indicate that Dostoevsky had intended to spawn another novel with Alyosha as the saintly believer going out into the whirling world rather than remaining behind inside the protective walls of the monastery or inside a cloud of mysticism. In Alyosha, Dostoevsky wanted to portray a young man preparing to show the practical, everyday side of love in action. In walking out of the monastery, Alyosha walks away from the sickly image of a Myshkin who teeters on the edge of losing his mind because the world conspires to crush him.

Even though Alyosha acts as the narrator's hero, the middle brother Ivan stands as the one who seems to trouble Dostoevsky the most. In some respects, he appears as the young Raskolnikov of *Crime and Punishment*. Dostoevsky has a strange affinity for Ivan Karamazov, the enemy who represents both the political and religious ideology that Dostoevsky sets out to demolish. Of all the heroes in the Dostoevsky novels, only Ivan Karamazov possesses the intellectual power equal to Dostoevsky's.

Ironically, in an August 24, 1879, letter to the powerful Konstantin Pobedonostsev, who would soon be appointed the chief procurator of the Holy Synod, Dostoevsky expressed deep concern that Ivan had stated his case with such force that Dostoevsky had not succeeded in answering his own creation (Mochulsky 590; Terras, *Companion* 41). In one of the most gripping passages of the entire novel, Dostoevsky commits perhaps a telling error by allowing Ivan to say, "I knew a robber in prison [who]... showed a strange affection for them [i.e., children] while he was in prison" (238; bk. 5, ch. 4).[1] Unlike Dostoevsky, Ivan in this story has never been in prison, but the account reads as if it were a first-hand experience. Is this passage a genuine Freudian slip, Dostoevsky identifying himself with Ivan at this point? In a May 10, 1879, letter to his editor, Nikolay Liubilov, Dostoevsky thrice refers to Ivan as "my hero."

> [Ivan's] convictions are precisely what I accept as the synthesis of Russian anarchism in our day: the denial not of God, but of the meaning of his creation. All socialism had its origins and beginnings in the denial of the meaning of historical actuality, and progressed to a program of destruction and anarchism. The original anarchists were in many cases men of sincere convictions. My hero takes up a topic I consider irrefutable: the senselessness of the suffering of children, and deduces from that the absurdness of all historical actuality. I don't know whether I carried it out well, but I know that the character of my hero is real in the highest degree. (In *The Possessed*, there were many characters they attacked me for as fantastic, but later, you believe me,...all [the characters] were justified by reality, so they must have been imagined correctly.)...All that my hero says in the text [that] I sent you is based on reality. All of the stories about children occurred, were printed in the papers, and I can show where: nothing was invented by me. (Belknap, *The Genesis* 128)

Three months later, in his August 10 letter to his editor, Dostoevsky still referred to Ivan as "my hero" and "the hero" (Krag 273).

---

[1]This particular passage has caused translators and commentators some difficulty. Pevear and Volokhonsky: "I knew a robber in prison..." Garnett: "I knew a criminal in prison..." Kjetsaa: "In prison I knew a robber...." We are following Geir Kjetsaa (338).

All references to the text of *The Brothers Karamazov* are from the Richard Pevear and Larissa Volokhonsky translation (North Point Press, 1990) and will be indicated by a parenthetical citation of the page number followed by the book number and chapter number.

Novelists have often said, and sometimes complained, that characters in their stories take over. It is a tempting hypothesis that Ivan, emerging in the creative process, literally pulled from Dostoevsky's subterranean Russian soul surging doubts, rival commitments, and clashing convictions, all of which became caught up in a vortex containing such power that they carried Dostoevsky along with them. Unquestionably, while writing *The Brothers Karamazov*, something happened to the great Russian novelist so that near the novel's completion, he was both the same man and a surprisingly different man. The novelist created both a work of art and a new dimension of himself. Ivan flew back upon his creator with a terrible vengeance. In the story, Ivan is like the Christ of the New Testament Apocalypse descending with a flaming sword. If Ivan is the terrifying genie in the novel, Dostoevsky set for himself the task of putting the genie back into the bottle. But did the bottle break in Dostoevsky's hand?

One story, perhaps apocryphal, states that Dostoevsky once said of himself and other contemporary Russian writers that they all came out of Gogol's overcoat, referring to Gogol's famous Russian short story "The Overcoat." From Dostoevsky's own overcoat, however, came a double creation, the terrible Ivan, who in turn creates the old cardinal in "The Legend of the Grand Inquisitor." The aged cardinal dares to confront Christ and accuse him of in effect betraying the human race. The atheism of the cardinal shakes the very foundation of Dostoevsky's faith. Dostoevsky feels deeply that unless he can counter the young man Ivan and his cardinal, he will fail in his greatest and most profound theodicy.

Drawing upon his past years of research and relentless thinking about the problem of human suffering, Dostoevsky calls into being a second elderly gentlemen, Zosima the Elder, to meet the challenge of Ivan and the old Grand Inquisitor. The Elder presents his audience with a theological framework that emerges from the Eastern Orthodox tradition and exemplifies genuinely new horizons that prove necessary in meeting the onslaught of atheism. *The Brothers Karamazov*, a superlative murder mystery, is also an ideological and theological war novel fought, Dostoevsky believed, in the human soul. (Perhaps to the surprise of no one, as soon as *The Brothers Karamazov* met with popular acclaim, some of the priests and theologians of Eastern Orthodoxy spoke against what they considered to be the Elder's seditious defense of the faith.)

To answer Ivan and his Grand Inquisitor, Dostoevsky creates in *The Brothers Karamazov* a laboratory in which to explore a way to account for the rise of human evil in the world. Through his experiments with the warring characters and intricate subplots in the novel, he reveals a startling theory that has far-reaching implications for social theory, moral philosophy, and metaphysics. Specifically, it links the origin of human evil with not only suffering and guilt, but also freedom, forgiveness, and human compassion.

Inside the laboratory, which sometimes approximates the model of an atomic reactor, appear such turbulent characters as the three brothers—Dmitri, Ivan, and Alyosha—and the embittered house servant Smerdyakov (possibly the fourth brother). The father, Fyodor Pavlovich Karamazov, ranks as one of the most despicable characters in literature. The novel teems with highly diverse personalities, each embodying an ideology lived to the fullest. Without the Elder Zosima, who lives in the monastery alongside the cynical young careerist Rakitin, the story would surely have taken an altogether different turn. Indeed, the laboratory contains a mini-laboratory, the monastery, a hot-bed of jealousy, pride, and contempt, all flourishing amid some of the most beautiful visions of love that the human mind can possess.

The story's subplots run the gamut from Madonna to Gomorrah, from filial affection and duty to patricide, from a morality rooted in faith and compassion to the amoralism of the reptile. The problem traditionally called theodicy permeates every chapter of the novel, so much so that it stands as one of the most daring attempts in all literature to look human evil and atrocity straight in the eye. So much attention has been devoted to Dostoevsky's so-called practical resolution of the problem of evil and suffering in *The Brothers Karamazov* that scholarly opinion has scarcely noticed what may well turn out to be the novel's most penetrating insight, namely, Dostoevsky's discovery of the origin of human evil.

The Brothers Karamazov's originality in dealing with the origin of human evil can best be brought out and explicated by comparing it with the views of three of Christianity's most influential theologians: Augustine, Pelagius, and Luther. Some comparisons with Darwinism and eventually with the metaphysics of personalism and process philosophy will also prove fruitful.

For Pelagius, the soul at birth stands clean and fresh, an unpolluted river fed only by the purest of streams. From that point forward, the soul enjoys the free will to choose the direction of its flow down either a channel of goodness or a channel of evil. For Augustine, two springs initially nourish the river: 1) beauty and goodness (the image of God) and 2) original evil. Pride and concupiscence block the flow of goodness, and the river becomes increasingly polluted. For Luther, only the evil source will feed the river until supernatural grace intervenes. After Adam, no individual has the freedom to choose either a course of goodness or one of evil.

Dostoevsky seems to have not only reformulated Augustine's doctrine of original sin, or original pride and sensuality, but also restricted it to the Karamazov men and a special number of Promethean families. It is both a kind of curse and a unique endowment.

The broader view of sin that prevails in *The Brothers Karamazov* may be characterized, not as original sin, but as original and inevitable conflict among finite mortals. The whole novel appears to serve as a laboratory designed to spell out this thesis in rich detail, showing not only the inevitability of the conflict but also the sin and immorality that conflict invariably generates. Earthly existence requires living in conflict and contradiction, and from this condition emerges human evil.

Paradoxically, the state of original conflict gives birth also to the possibility of human freedom and the love that freedom makes possible. Specifically, without conflict, no suffering would occur; and without suffering, apparently no occasion for human love would emerge. Between the suffering and the possibility of love lies freedom, without which human love would amount to nothing more than the instinctive affection exemplified by animals to their young and to their mates. In *The Brothers Karamazov*, the cockroach and the insect represent blind passion and sensuality below the level of freedom and love. Only human beings can move beyond reaction to the point of free action. Consequently, the fall of humankind emerges in the state of conflict that allows humankind to rise above the animal. The fall and the ascendance go hand in hand.

For Ivan Karamazov, the original conflict generates such overwhelming suffering and agony, especially for children, that he deems the world unworthy of God. Alyosha, by contrast, believes that the only answer to the suffering arising from the conflict is the unifying power of love. In some respects, these are not so much two rival answers as two *kinds* of responses to the problem. Unquestionably, Alyosha's beloved mentor, the Elder Zosima, envisions a utopia in the form of a *com*-unity that will somehow so overcome all estrangement, alienation, and conflict that all the contradictions and clashes of earthly existence will eventually be justified and will manifest the beauty and goodness of the Creator. For Dostoevsky, life cannot be life without passion—"the sticky little leaves...[and] the blue sky" (230; bk. 5, ch. 3). In short, it must have richness of content. Any unity that drains off the passion and richness of life is a mere anemic abstraction, a ballet of bloodless categories worthy of neither God nor his free creatures. Conflict and suffering, therefore, enrich the whole. The suffering in *The Brothers Karamazov*, neither a hapless nor an expendable byproduct, belongs to God's world; and without it, creation as a whole would be less beautiful and good.

Dostoevsky's theory of original conflict has stunning implications for the nature of God. A line of thought not hitherto spelled out in any depth in the Dostoevsky literature, the theory of original conflict makes poignant inroads not only into the Christian doctrine of atonement, to which Dostoevsky offers genuinely penetrating insight, but also into the doctrine of incarnation, with which the Eastern Church in particular has wrestled for centuries.

Much has been written about Dostoevsky's view of freedom, but the connection between freedom and original conflict requires systematic analysis. Dostoevsky's radical notion of freedom enters uncompromisingly into his doctrine of God. The systematic pursuit of the theological implication of freedom has for over a hundred years stood in need of bold explication.

Chapter II. Three Views of the Origin of Sin

The brilliance of Dostoevsky's concept of original conflict becomes apparent when placed against the backdrop of the following three views of the origin of sin:

- *Pelagius'* conviction that sin accrues from social habit, not from an inherently bad nature,

- *Augustine's* contention that sin originates in everyone through biological transmission, though some goodness in the form of the image of God remains, and

■   *Luther's* belief that everyone after Adam
     inherits a totally sinful nature.

The particular way in which each of these men, as well as Dostoevsky, defines the
origin of sin seems to impact his view of other critical matters, such as free will,
the image of God, divine grace, pride, and concupiscence.

Two ancient views of human depravity, *distributed* versus *absolute*, form
a foundation for contrasting the opinions of Pelagius, Augustine, and Luther on the
origin of sin. According to distributed depravity, sin touches and infects every
aspect of human life. Corruption permeates not only the entire race, including
every individual, but every aspect of each individual's life. No part of human
existence, including body and soul, escapes the plague of sin.

According to the doctrine of absolute corruption, on the other hand, not
only does depravity stain every facet of human life, but it corrupts every aspect to
the fullest, leaving no thread of goodness, and blowing out like a candle whatever
goodness once existed in the human race. Nothing remains but the absolute and
total darkness of sin. Not only is there none righteous, no not one, but the spark
of righteousness has been obliterated from human nature.

Unfortunately, the world has been deprived of many of Pelagius' writings
because of his condemnation by Bishop Zosimus of Rome in C.E. 416
(Lehmann 205). We know that he was a monk, British or perhaps Irish, "of
excellent repute, much learning, and great moral earnestness, who had settled in
Rome.... With the East generally, and in agreement with many in the West, he
held to the freedom of the human will. 'If I ought, I can,' well expresses his
position" (Walker 185).

Although he portrays evil as widely distributed throughout many if not
most members of the human race, Pelagius seems to disagree with both of the two
ancient doctrines of depravity: distributed depravity and absolute corruption.
According to Williston Walker, Pelagius "recognized that the mass of men are
bad. Adam's sin set them an ill example, which they have been quick to follow.
Hence they almost all need to be set right" (185-6). Nevertheless, on the question
of human depravity and free will, Pelagius and the African bishop Augustine lock
horns. According to Pelagius, the pervasiveness of human sin around the world
comes about through the misuse of the individual's free will. He questions the
rationale behind holding people morally responsible for what they lack the capacity

to achieve. Consequently, he sees mankind as born with a free will so powerful that each individual can always choose to go either in the direction of goodness and holiness or in the direction of evil and corruption. Sin pervades the world not because of some primitive deposit of evil in the stream of human life, but because over the years each individual has chosen immorality and in so doing has personally accumulated a backlog of evil.

Pelagius apparently believed that Augustine had generated a doctrine of original sin that caused two severe theological problems. First, he viewed Augustinianism as undercutting free will and therefore human responsibility. Second, he thought Augustinianism unwittingly made God the culprit. If mankind is born without the capacity for both choosing a life of holiness and rejecting immorality, the pervasiveness of evil lies at the Creator's doorstep (Lehmann 211).

A somewhat atomistic view of the self lies in the background of Pelagius' idea of sin, the opposite of the position taken by Father Zosima in Dostoevsky's *The Brothers Karamazov*. As a radical pluralist, Pelagius views the individual as relatively disconnected from other individuals. This is true, however, only in one crucial respect. Without denying that each individual's life has far-reaching impact on the lives of others, Pelagius seems to assume that the individual, a moral island, must harbor his or her own responsibility for holiness. Otherwise, the whole idea of culpability and righteousness will break down. For Pelagius, righteousness is radically individualized. The human race does not sin, but individuals do. Immorality spreads when individuals deny moral responsibility for their own sins and shift blame to others. From mankind's pagan past had come the bad "social habit" of misplacing culpability, which resulted in the pain felt in the world (Brown 349). Pelagius finds morally repulsive Augustine's idea of treating the entire human race as one individual smeared with collective guilt.

Like Augustine, Pelagius holds that God created each human in his own image. For Pelagius, however, this image endures unobstructed after the Fall, for nothing exemplifies the divine image more than free will, a capacity unique to humans because God created no other species in his image.

The analogy of a river coursing its way through the terrain can throw considerable light on the similarities and differences among Pelagius, Augustine, Luther, and eventually Dostoevsky. For Pelagius, each human, like a self-directing river, determines his or her own course. Veering in one direction, a person chooses to run through the terrain of holiness and righteousness, making the river itself increasingly pure and sanctified. Electing the opposite course, however, guides one's life through the terrain of vileness, perversity, and corruption. In time, this direction succeeds only in polluting the river, making it more difficult, though never impossible, to change course. The possibility of changing directions is the image of God in all its force. Without this possibility, the image of God is, for Pelagius, mere words.

Williston Walker states that Pelagius did embrace the concept of grace, "but to him grace was remission of sins in baptism and general divine teaching. To Augustine the main work of grace was that infusion of love by which character is gradually transformed" (186). Consequently, in their theological quarrel, Pelagius and Augustine disagreed not about the existence of divine grace, but about the way grace and human freedom interacted. For Pelagius, divine grace could never replace free will, but rather showed itself to be grace by respecting free will. Grace lies, at the same time, always available for both sinners and believers. It functions as the available terrain of goodness through which the river may travel. In doing so, the river receives from grace all the purity and goodness that Christian doctrine has extolled. Grace, however, does not determine the path the river will take. Grace is not irresistible.

Pelagius disagreed vehemently with Augustine on the issue of the biological transmission of sin through the sexual act. Paul Lehmann notes that Pelagius saw as contrary to everyday experience the idea that infants sin.

> To focus the whole human and religious problem upon a biologically transmitted predisposition of sin...not only undermined the theory and practice of infant baptism but called in question the institution of marriage as well. (212)

Pelagius' principal opponent, St. Augustine (C.E. 354—C.E. 430), a North African, "the father of Latin Theology, the progenitor of the major ideas and terminology of medieval Catholicism,...is also a kind of spiritual grandfather to Luther and the Protestant Reformers, whom he profoundly influenced" (Cole 43). According to Peter Brown, St. Augustine wrote his *Confessions* as an "analysis of the 'heart'," in which he states that he had witnessed jealousy and anger even in innocent-looking babies. Their innocence stemmed not from a lack of will, but from a lack of strength (28-9).

Augustine portrays the human race as a "'mass of perdition'" (Walker 181). In some sense, he views the first couple as the whole human race, so that when Adam and Eve sinned, the human race sinned. In *The City of God*, Augustine writes, "Among the terrestrial animals man was made by Him in His own image, and...was made one individual, though he was not left alone. For there is nothing so social by nature, so unsocial by its corruption, as this race" (*The City of God* 359). More specifically, Augustine advances the distributive version of depravity. Every human being is born into sin and is guilty. This is original sin. Augustine did not, however, embrace the notion of absolute corruption in the sense that each aspect of every individual stands one hundred percent corrupt. All the same, the weight of depravity presses so heavily that no sinner can of his or her own initiative change course. While there remains a perpetual restlessness in the individual as a testimony to a life better than perversity, no one can embark on a life of holiness and goodness apart from supernatural intervention from heaven.

Augustine rejects Pelagius' doctrine that one can be held responsible only for what one is capable of achieving. Augustine appears to embrace both a doctrine of free will and a doctrine of original sin that severely thwarts free will. Some interpreters see Augustine as a theologian of paradox at this point. His doctrine of predestination clearly comes down on the side of divine initiative, whereas Pelagius leaves initiative with the human individual. To be sure, for Pelagius, the original deposit of free will is a divine work; but it remains an essential part of the "natural man." For Augustine, the "natural man" is in some sense no longer natural, but perverse because of Adam's sin.

If original sin brought about by the First Adam does in some way cause every individual thereafter to participate in sin to the point of depravity leading to damnation, what can be said of Augustine's notion of free will? Here the plot thickens. Aware that if he surrenders the doctrine of free will he will leave the cause of human sin at the doorstep of the Creator, Augustine tries to retain both free will and the majesty and goodness of God. He appears also to hold to the crucial importance of free will, not simply in rendering human beings responsible for their sins, but in advancing love. Without free will, human creatures could not love either God or other human beings; and human achievement would rise no higher than that of animal affection and desire. As will be discussed later, Dostoevsky's Father Zosima embraces a view quite similar to this, but with profoundly important shades of difference.

Augustine's complicated, if not contradictory, doctrine of free will is incomprehensible apart from his view of the image of God in every person. Like Pelagius, he holds that human beings reflect the image of God. Also, with Pelagius, he regards free will as an element of that image.

Augustine elaborates on the image of God, seeing it as in some sense a reflection of the Trinity. The human self exemplifies a trinity of "memory, understanding, will, or the even more famous lover, loved, and love" (Walker 180). For Augustine, without the image of God in his beloved creature, no residue would abide to be saved. Even after the Fall, human beings are, after all, still human beings, not animals. The image of God in individuals causes each to suffer guilt after sinning. Sensing that their lives after the Fall veer from their true destiny and fulfillment, sinners, thanks to the image of God, see that they have only a temporal, imperfect life, even though God created them for eternity. Even when sinning, the individual cannot wholly thrive in sin, for the image of God generates a restlessness, a divine discontent. The life of the profligate Dmitri vividly exemplifies this theme in Dostoevsky's *The Brothers Karamazov*.

In Augustine's theology, pride appears as the most far-reaching and damning of sins. William Cole notes that Augustine in *The City of God* views original sin not as the sexual act, but "pride, which he defined as 'a perverse desire of elevation, forsaking Him to whom the soul ought to cleave as its beginning, and the making of one's self the one beginning'" (Cole 48). Pride, the sin of Adam and Eve, appears to turn even human sexuality into unchecked lust and conquest.

Unfortunately, pride seems to have many meanings in Augustine's thoughts. One meaning appears to be a loss of perspective about oneself. In other words, in pride, the opposite of humility, a person makes claims that elevate him or her inordinately in the Great Chain of Being. The chief sin seems to be that of elevating oneself to the position of God. This inappropriate status-juggling is defiance of one's position under God and the Church. Unbelief is the chief mark of pride for Augustine, who treats it as not mere suspension of belief or honest doubt, but belief in oneself as a God. When he condemns self-love as sinful, Augustine seems to imply that the sin lies in loving a distorted image of the self so that the sin becomes not so much love per se, but love misdirected.

Etienne Gilson interprets Augustine on this issue as follows. The soul loses track of itself only if it fails to place itself according to nature and on the proper level of the chain of cosmic order (i.e., above bodies and beneath God).

> But as soon as it claims to be self-sufficient and to be responsible itself for the perfection it can receive only from God, it turns away from God towards the corporeal. The more it claims to grow in perfection the more it decreases, because once separated from God, its sole sufficiency, it cannot find sufficiency in itself, nor can any other thing satisfy it. (*Christian Philosophy* 99)

Furthermore, Gilson states that for Augustine separation from God would cause the soul to live in constant turmoil, always seeking fulfillment but never attaining it.

> Although aware that the knowledge of the sensible will not meet its needs, it busies itself therewith, becomes dissatisfied even with the pleasure it derives therefrom, looks for other things which also fail to satisfy and which leave it rather hungrier than before and exhausts itself in a giddy pursuit of things which excite desire but fail to satisfy it. (*Christian Philosophy* 99)

Finally, according to Gilson, Augustine believed that the image of God in the soul becomes clouded when the soul is enslaved by the excess of sensations. The pursuit of satisfaction, when deprived of God, turns sour.

> It [the soul] is present and vaguely known; it sees itself dimly through the veil of sensations which hide its true nature and simply tries to see itself more clearly. (*Christian Philosophy* 100)

Concupiscence[1] and lust for Augustine sometimes appear to be sexual desire itself, which means that Augustine condemns natural passion. Another interpretation, however, suggests that much of what troubled Augustine personally about sexual passion was its tendency to exalt itself over all else, thus making itself a god with a license to dominate and rule. When Augustine speaks of lust out of the control of reason, this may be interpreted to mean sexual passion unbridled, disconnected from the remaining human drives. According to William Cole, after the Fall, Adam and Eve no longer had "control of all of their faculties... . They were still able to control and direct their arms and legs and eyes, but their sexual organs acted independently ..." (49-50). For Augustine, the "covering...of sensation with which it has become overlaid" obstructs the soul from seeing "its own nature" (Gilson, *Christian Philosophy* 100). It is important to understand that even when a Manichee, Augustine had difficulty with lust. Apparently this was no academic problem only, but a personal crisis that he perhaps never resolved in his lifetime. *The Brothers Karamazov* is a literary laboratory in which intense personal struggles like Augustine's are vividly played out in the concrete lives of especially Dmitri, Ivan, and Alyosha.

In Augustine's scheme, pride appears with an ontological or metaphysical undertow. On the one hand, it is an attempt to step out of one's ontological place in the Great Chain of Being, while, on the other hand, it is a slide toward non-being. Here the monism of Augustine's earlier Neoplatonism comes into full play. Unwilling to follow the dualistic Manichees by giving evil a genuine ontological status independent of the God of Light, he was compelled by his mixture of monotheism and Neoplatonism to view evil as a derivative reality at best. He concludes that pride and all other sins infected by it are fundamentally a distancing of the soul from God (Goodness). Williston Walker elaborates:

> Man, according to Augustine, was created good and upright, possessed of free will, endowed with the possibility of not sinning and of immortality. There was no discord in his nature. He was happy and in communion with God. From this state

---

[1]On the function of concupiscence in Augustine's thought, Jeremy Cohen offers important insights (507).

Adam fell by sin, the essence of which was pride. Its
consequence was the loss of good. (181)

If evil cannot under the rule of an omnipotent God obtain positive (i.e.,
actual) status, it can only have for Augustine the status of being derived from
goodness but nevertheless not participating in goodness. Augustine in defiance of
his earlier Manichaeism seems forced to say that creation itself is good; therefore,
if this is true, the existence of evil in the scheme of things must in some sense be
good even though evil itself is never good. Augustine calls evil the deprivation of
good; that is, goodness in a deprived and alien state, but nevertheless somehow a
part of overall goodness. This concept emerges in *The Brothers Karamazov* when
Ivan speaks of the ultimate harmony of all the contradictions. For Augustine, the
contradictions are a part of the good, and yet for all that, sin is sufficient to damn
great masses of human souls to endless torment. For Augustine, hell is the agony
of the divine restlessness in the individual, a torment that never gains relief, but
endures forever. Etienne Gilson interprets Augustine as follows:

> Hidden somewhere in the memory must be the assurance that
> unless it [the soul] knows itself, it will never reach a certain goal
> which it ought to reach, a goal consequently of great excellence,
> namely peace, perfect security, in a word, happiness.
> (*Christian Philosophy* 100)

For Augustine, lust in the great scheme of things turns out to be a type
of theo-alchemy whereby sin as a disease of the soul is transmitted to the next
generation, a spiritual Lamarckism that transmits original sin. The image of God
is also transmitted in some sense, but the goodness and grace that comes through
the baptism of the parents is not transmitted by the parents but only through the
means of the Church.

Augustine affirms both prevenient grace and irresistible grace. He
believes that the two doctrines fit hand in glove with the doctrine of original sin,
the last doctrine leaving individuals lacking the ability to direct their lives into the
territory of righteousness. For Augustine, an individual is not a self-directing
river that can at will turn its course. Rather, the river comes already flowing.
Into it pour from the beginning pure springs, which Augustine labels "the image
of God." After the Fall, however, pride, concupiscence, and all the other sins

pour in as pollutants to contaminate the river. The self is no longer pristine, but infected to the point that the sinner can no longer initiate repentance.

Augustine at this point is attempting to solve more than one problem; but in solving one, he creates more difficulties for the others. The problem is to explain the apparent loss that the Creator would experience in knowing that great masses will be doomed forever. If this doom extends beyond the pale of divine providence, however, so that God does not in some way bring it about, God's position as the Supreme governor of the universe comes into question. Providence itself suffers a crack in the dike. By design, therefore, the doctrine of prevenient and irresistible grace is a desperate effort to maintain the doctrine of omnipotent Providence. Augustine could not bring himself to say that evil slipped somehow from the control of God or that it happened behind God's back without his awareness and will.

Predestination follows, Augustine appears to think, from the tenets of divine providence and omnipotence. In short, God not only knows what will happen so that nothing surprises him, but he foreordains all. If he foreordains all, he foreordains salvation for some and damnation for others. For God to avoid playing catch-up with his own creation, prevenient grace becomes necessary. The bishop cannot concede that Providence must wait upon human initiative before salvation can have a chance. Williston Walker explains Augustine's view as follows:

> This grace comes to those to whom God chooses to send it. He therefore predestinates whom He will, "to punishment and to salvation." The number of each class is fixed. Augustine had held, in the period immediately following his conversion, that it is in man's power to accept or reject grace, but even before the Pelagian controversy, he had come to the conclusion that grace is irresistible. (182)

Indeed, in Augustine's world, chance has no existence. All is of God, all planned, foreknown and predestined. God predestines not only his own eternal ends, but all the means and instruments by which the ends are to be attained. Free will, therefore, comes within the providence of God so that the will itself, which

lies latent in human nature as a component of the image of God, can activate only if touched by prevenient grace. But prevenient grace is also irresistible grace.

> Therefore assistance was bestowed on the weakness of man's will, that it might be unalterably and irresistibly influenced by divine grace; and that, weak as it was, it might still not fail nor be overcome by any adversity. So it came about that man's will, when weak and powerless, and as yet in a lowly state of good, still persevered, by God's strength, in that good; while the will of the first man, though strong and healthy, possessed of the power of free choice, and in a state of greater good, did not persevere in that good.... For them that were weak he reserved his own gift whereby they should [both] irresistibly will what is good, and irresistibly refuse to forsake it. (*De correptione et gratia* 79)

Because of passages such as the above, some critics have accused Augustine of falling into irrevocable contradiction, while others have praised him for generating creative insights even though he could not fully reconcile the insights in his own mind. Augustine set for himself the task of holding on to absolute sovereignty, omnipotence, and omniscience for the Creator, on the one hand, and free will for the human creature made in the deity's image, on the other hand. In the end, perhaps *Augustine defined freedom more as unimpeded activity than as choice*, since the unimpeded activity harmonizes more easily with the doctrine of predestination (*City of God* 617). In this way, once irresistible grace sets the elect on their course, they can proceed to their blissful end without fatal impediment from the powers of evil.

Though influenced strongly by Augustine, *Martin Luther,* some 1100 years after Augustine's death, embraced the *absolute depravity* view. Entering an Augustinian monastery in 1505 twelve years after his German birth, Luther sought to overcome the effect of two significant experiences: "the sudden death of a friend and...a narrow escape from lightning.." (Walker 337). While in the monastery, he developed his belief that mankind, a totally depraved species, had no free will from which to choose goodness. Ironically, some twelve years later, with no rebellious intention, the monk Luther stimulated the Protestant Reformation by pinning his "ninety-five theses on the theory and practice of indulgences" to the door of the Castle church in Wittenburg (Cole 100). He died in 1546, saddened that "the preaching of justification by faith" had not transformed "the social, civic, and political life about him..." (Walker 379).

For the Protestant reformer of Germany, every member of the human race is corrupted in every aspect of life and to the fullest. Adam and Eve infected the entire human race, Adam serving as something of a federal head representing all. The Natural Man after the Fall does evil because it is his nature. Indeed, for some Protestant scholars in Luther's tradition, the sin of the human race spread out across the earth and entered the animal kingdom.

According to Luther, even though mankind can create social good in the practical sense on earth, in the eyes of God human goodness counts for nothing since it rises from the sin of pride. All our deeds of righteousness are as filthy rags (Luther 296, 312).

For Luther, free will after the Fall is in bondage. The individual's rescue from total depravity requires an act initiated outside human nature. The river at the source was pure and untainted, but once the pollutants, beginning with Adam, poured into the river, all was lost. Not even one clear stream of free will remains, which means that no individual has any power to initiate a life of goodness. Only a supernatural influx of grace can create free will in the fallen creature (Luther 104-5).

Natural Man after the Fall walks in the gloom of depravity without one flicker of the divine image. "Nature, reason, intellect, works, all failed..." (Marty 215). If for Augustine the divine image in fallen man is distorted, for Luther it is annihilated. Every move toward righteous goals is corrupted and completely without merit. For all practical purposes, the Natural Man, wholly without worth and his doom certain, stands without hope (Luther 317).

For Luther, divine grace is an act of creation, not merely a cleansing process. The sinner, having nothing to commend himself or herself, lacks all capacity to initiate any change leading to God. Grace, therefore, must ***create*** the capacity itself. And this process is close to creation out of nothing. Discriminatory election obviously follows, since many go unsaved. Luther professed not to know why God chose some to receive mercy and others damnation. It is ultimately and inexplicably of God's own free will in grace (Luther 314-15).

Luther seemed to look at the caste system implied in Augustine's Neoplatonism as a form of sinful pride. He shook the Great Chain of Being. This is not to say that Luther advanced a democratic view of the state, but rather that he advanced a view that allowed the believers to regard their calling as sacred. He gave no special awards to the life of celibacy or monasticism. Christians were called to live in the world and to function in the world. Luther believed that "the normal trades and occupations of life" were essentially good and that "all believers are priests" (Walker 344). This doctrine appears to have influenced Dostoevsky to such an extent that the Elder Zosima urges his disciple Alyosha to leave the monastery in order to do his good deeds in the world (77; bk. 2, ch. 7). The Elder has a very complicated and subtle position on the monastic life that is neither Augustine's nor Luther's position. In the monastery, Dostoevsky graphically portrays the pride of Father Ferapont, showing how pride infects the life purported to be dedicated to the cultivation of humility (163-71; bk. 4, ch. 1).

A mixed bag, Luther's view of concupiscence and lust eventually transcends itself by portraying marriage as a high calling and putting no stock in celibacy. The place of sexuality beyond the purpose of procreation and in the overall economy of God, however, becomes lost in obscurity if not contradiction.

While steeped in the Christian heritage, Dostoevsky's view of the origin of sin is a genuinely new contribution to that tradition. Unlike Pelagius, Dostoevsky believes in some form of biological transmission of sin, but he confines it to the special case of Karamazovism. Unlike Augustine and Luther, Dostoevsky, by not creating a gap between nature and grace, affirms the human ability to influence the good and evil contents of the river.

Chapter III. Karamazovism: A Curse and a Blessing

Throughout *The Brothers Karamazov*, a phenomenon appears that deserves the term "Karamazovism," a curse and a blessing that distinguish some families of the human race from all other members. Professor Victor Terras defines it as "a faculty for going 'all the way' in everything" (*Companion* 102). Robert Belknap defines it as the thirst for life combined with the capacity for vileness (*Structure* 30). According to F. F. Seely, at heart the Karamazov brothers have a stormy passion for life, but they are not voluptuaries like Fyodor, whose lusts have devoured his ability to love (123, 125). Ironically, the blood inherited from Fyodor flows within the three Karamazov brothers whose Karamazovism represents an intensified condensation of Dostoevsky's beloved Russian people.

The essence of Karamazovism lies in the individual's having an excessive endowment of humanity, including pride and concupiscence. Karamazovism, the curse of being human in all its wildness and unrestrained passion, appears not so much the curse of original sin portrayed by Augustine or Luther as the curse of receiving the full cup of life from which to drink. In itself neither wholly good nor wholly evil, Karamazovism comprises the full potential for either in all its fury. The oldest brother, Dmitri, says to Alyosha, the youngest:

> "And all of us Karamazovs are like that, and in you, an angel, the same insect [of sensuality] lives and stirs up storms in your blood. Storms, because sensuality is a storm, more than a storm! Beauty is a fearful and terrible thing! Fearful because it's undefinable, and it cannot be defined, because here God gave us only riddles." (108; bk. 3, ch. 3)

Significantly, this confession from the mouth of Dmitri occurs in the chapter entitled "The Confession of an Ardent Heart. In Verse," located in Book Three entitled "The Sensualists." By identifying the Karamazovs with the insect, Dmitri focuses on pre-rational passion or sensuality, life before the constraints of the intellect have come upon it, life in the raw stage and without evaluation. Dmitri uses beauty to describe this sensuality both in its intensity and scope. In scope, it ranges from the ideal of the Madonna to the ideal of Sodom. The heart blazes with both ideals, so much so that Dmitri cries out:

> "No, man is broad, even too broad, I would narrow him down. Devil knows even what to make of him, that's the thing! What's shame for the mind is beauty all over for the heart." (108; bk. 3, ch. 3)

In the pre-rational heart, beauty exists even in Sodom, for it embraces not only fear, but also mystery. The heart emerges as the battlefield where the Devil struggles with God (108; bk. 3, ch. 3).

Karamazovism, life in its extremities, a laceration, an unbridled energy that teems to the point of erupting from within, contains all human contradictions and absurdities. Ivan describes this phenomenon when he tells Alyosha:

"And observe, that cruel people—passionate, carnivorous, Karamazovian—sometimes love children very much.... I knew a robber in prison: he happened, in the course of his career, while slaughtering whole families in the houses he broke into and robbed at night, to have put the knife to several children as well. But he showed a strange affection for them while he was in prison." (238; bk. 5, ch. 4)

Karamazovism contrasts with its exact opposite, the Laodicean syndrome of lukewarmness, of being neither hot nor cold, for which the Christ of the New Testament Apocalypse spews the Laodicean Church out of his mouth (Rev. 3:15). No Laodicean, Alyosha always loves in an active manner that cannot bear uncertainty (187; bk. 4, ch. 5). According to the Protestant theologian Daniel Williams, Augustine thought that understanding required belief (6). Likewise, according to the Roman Catholic philosopher Etienne Gilson, Augustine saw understanding as the reward of faith (*Reason* 19). If Augustine meant by belief whole-hearted commitment and passionate devotion, the Karamazovism exhibited in Alyosha stems from Augustinian roots. Thus, Karamazovism harbors not only the depravity, cruelty and shame that Dmitri professes as his lot, but the love that the oldest son believes God foreordained for Alyosha. Believing that he, too, participates in the extremes of Karamazovism, Alyosha tells Dmitri that they are the same.

> [Dmitri asks,] "You? Well, that's going a bit too far."
> "No, not too far," Alyosha said hotly. (Apparently the thought had been with him for some time.) "The steps are the same. I'm on the lowest, and you are above, somewhere on the thirteenth. That's how I see it, but it's all one and the same, all exactly the same sort of thing. Whoever steps on the lowest step will surely step on the highest."
> "So one had better not step at all."
> "Not if one can help it."
>
> "Can you?"
> "It seems not." (109-10; bk. 3, ch. 4)

Apparently, Alyosha agrees with Dmitri that Karamazovism is bestowed upon some but not all members of the human race.

The Brothers Karamazov does not reveal Alyosha as one given to cruelty, shame, and depravity. While Alyosha's doubts after the Elder's "odor of corruption" prime him for an evening of debauchery at Grushenka's, his brief plunge ends abruptly the minute Grushenka shows him the slightest empathy.

> "The elder Zosima died!" Grushenka exclaimed.
> "Oh, Lord, I didn't know!" She crossed herself piously.
> "Lord, but what am I doing now, sitting on his lap!" She
> suddenly gave a start as if in fright, jumped off his knees at
> once, and sat down on the sofa. Alyosha gave her a long,
> surprised look, and something seemed to light up in his face.
> (351; bk. 7, ch. 3)

Commenting that he had come to Grushenka's "looking for a wicked soul," Alyosha concludes that he instead "found a true sister...a loving soul" (351; bk. 7, ch. 3). This would seem to suggest that he does not participate fully in Karamazovism. To draw this conclusion, however, would be premature. Dostoevsky himself makes it clear in "From the Author" immediately before plunging into the story that while he has only one "biography," with Alyosha as its hero, he has two novels: the first, *The Brothers Karamazov*; the second, a future saga to take place thirteen years after the first. Unfortunately, Dostoevsky died before completing his vision of the "main novel" (3; "From the Author"). According to a March 25, 1870, letter written by Dostoevsky, he planned to write a novel as large and sweeping as *War and Peace*, with *The Brothers Karamazov* apparently serving as an earlier stage of this vision ("To Apollan" 190-2). In a March 24, 1870, letter, he proposed to title the sweeping novel "The Life-Story of a Great Sinner" ("To Nikolay" 187).

In some ways, for a life at the Karamazov level of wildness (i.e., untamed wilderness), all things are possible, everything lawful, for there is no law, no logos, "no meaning."

> "There is a force that will endure everything," said
> Ivan, this time with a cold smirk.

"What force?" [asked Alyosha.]

"The Karamazov force...the force of the Karamazov baseness."

"To drown in depravity, to stifle your soul with corruption, is that it?"

"That, too, perhaps...only until my thirtieth year maybe I'll escape it, and then..."

"How will you escape it? By means of what? With your thoughts, it's impossible."

"Again, in Karamazov fashion."

"You mean 'everything is permitted'? Everything is permitted, is that right, is it?"

(263; bk. 5, ch. 5)

Yet, ironically, this primordial surge brings meaning to life, for without it, existence fades into abstraction and passionless nonentity. The middle brother, Ivan, insists that from his cup, this life of the blue sky and the sticky leaves in the spring, he will drink until at least the age of thirty.

"I've asked myself many times: is there such despair in the world as could overcome this wild and perhaps indecent thirst for life in me, and have decided that apparently there is not—that is, once again, until my thirtieth year, after which I myself shall want no more, so it seems to me." (230; bk. 5, ch. 3)

Evidently, the Karamazov storm has enveloped Ivan. Even though Dmitri sometimes emphasizes the Karamazov curse as one of lechery and baseness, Ivan calls it the thirst for life and says to Alyosha that it resides in him, too. For that reason, Ivan does not reduce it to baseness, but calls it a centrifugal force on our planet and identifies it with the sticky leaves, the blue sky, persons whom he cherishes, and with the love of some "without even knowing why" (230; bk. 5, ch. 3). Even if no logic supports wanting to continue living, "to honor one's heart" Ivan will go on despite logic. Alyosha agrees:

"I understand it all too well, Ivan: to want to love with your insides, your guts—you said it beautifully, and I'm terribly glad that you want so much to live.... I think that everyone should love life before everything else in the world." (230-31; bk. 5, ch. 3)

To this, Ivan asks, "Love life more than its meaning?" (231; bk. 5, ch. 3) In one of his most philosophical moments, Alyosha states that love supersedes logic, and that only then can one understand the meaning of life. Ivan and Alyosha agree on this first half. On the second half, the resurrection, a continued existence and a never-extinguished thirst for life, Ivan disagrees. One part of him does not believe in the order of life; that is, he cannot fully embrace Alyosha's expectation of immortality. At the same time, a part of him does believe in the ongoing of life, but he refuses to approve of it because the contradictions and wildness bring too much suffering, especially to the children:

"It's not God that I do not accept, you understand, it is this world of God's, created by God, that I do not accept and cannot agree to accept. With one reservation: I have a childlike conviction that the sufferings will be healed and smoothed over, that the whole offensive comedy of human contradictions will disappear like a pitiful mirage, a vile concoction of man's Euclidean mind, feeble and puny as an atom, and that ultimately, at the world's finale, in the moment of eternal harmony, there will occur and be revealed something so precious that it will suffice for all hearts, to allay all indignation, to redeem all human villainy, all bloodshed; it will suffice not only to make forgiveness possible, but also to justify everything that has happened with men—let this, let all this come true and be revealed, but I do not accept it and do not want to accept it! Let the parallel lines even meet before my own eyes: I shall look and say, yes, they meet, and still I will not accept it. That is my essence, Alyosha, that is my thesis." (235-6; bk. 5, ch. 3)

Ironically, Alyosha's gospel of immortality itself exemplifies Karamazovism, life at the extremities, going all the way. Despite Ivan's skepticism, the murder of their father, the shameless bickering and envy in the monastery, and all the other outrageous slings and arrows unveiled in the novel, Alyosha emphatically maintains, "Certainly we shall rise, certainly we shall see and gladly, joyfully tell one another all that has been" (776; "Epilogue," ch. 3). This means that more than Ivan or Dmitri, Alyosha is truly the novel's hero just because he is more fully a Karamazov. The depth and scope of his Karamazov nature develops, however, only partially in *The Brothers Karamazov*, which became the first of two novels Dostoevsky had promised to write about his young hero. Death overtook Dostoevsky before he could write the second novel.

Rakitin, a somewhat cynical seminarian with expediency as his modus operandi, looks upon Karamazovism as lechery, murder, and baseness. Indeed, according to Michael Holquist, Rakitin affirms a proto-Freudian doctrine of the primal horde when he says to Alyosha that his house stinks of crime. Embodying sensuality and a devouring fever, Fyodor, the Karamazovs' father and a tribal despot, dominates his sons and mistreats their mothers (178-80).

Dmitri, on the other hand, contends that although "base and vile," he still carries the capacity to love God and to enjoy, since he is a child of God (107; bk. 3, ch. 3). For Dmitri, Karamazovism means falling into the abyss, heels up, pleased to fall, finding beauty in his humiliation. At the very moment of shame, however, he begins a hymn. Despite his vileness, he kisses the hem that clothes God. Though following the Devil, he prays, "I am also your son, Lord, and I love you, and I feel a joy without which the world cannot stand and be" (107; bk. 3, ch. 3). Ivan insists that the world stands on absurdities and contradictions. Dmitri, while not denying Ivan's view, adds that the world cannot stand without joy. For him, joy functions as the mainspring of the whole, the brimming cup.

To think of the Karamazov storm as welling up solely from within individuals as if they led isolated, insulated lives would be a mistake. Life, and therefore baseness and love, can spring into existence only through interaction and interrelationships. Karamazovism, a family curse, gives rise to the possibility of both damnation and salvation. **When people fail to transform life's interactions into love, they experience damnation on earth.** A second mistake, however, comes from thinking of love as some kind of essence that the individual either

inhales or exudes. It is nothing if not **a way of relating and interacting, a way of confessing, forgiving, and, above all, of being forgiven.** Forgiveness begins with confessing one's pride and baseness and ends with the restoration to good favor.

Father Zosima, who perhaps represents more than anyone Dostoevsky's own theological perspective, insists that the believer must beg the forgiveness of birds and other creatures of the earth, since love requires an all-inclusive relationship with the world. When Zosima's brother insists that he finds life a paradise, he has in mind the recognition of all creatures as manifestations of divine glory and the acceptance of such creatures in the spirit of forgiveness and humility. "Let me be sinful before everyone, but so that everyone will forgive me, and that is paradise. Am I not in paradise now?" (290; bk. 6, ch. 2)

Dostoevsky's metaphysics, intimately binding God and creation, leans much more toward pantheism—or, as we will show in a later chapter, pane*n*theism or personalism—than toward the sharp dualism of the Western Church. Dostoevsky appears to view the earth as in some sense an incarnation of God and the Russian people and the soil itself as a special repository of divinity. In an earlier novel, Dostoevsky develops more thoroughly the theme of Russia as the "only God-bearing nation on earth, destined to regenerate and save the world" (**The Possessed** 234; pt. 2, ch. 1).[1]   Karamazovism represents a special condensation of the Russian people, a more intensified version that reveals Russian extremes. Therefore, both a curse and a blessing, Karamazovism acts as the full repository of life itself, God's greatest gift.

The logic of Dostoevsky's metaphysics progresses from the world in general to Russia and then to full-blown Karamazovism.[2] As if Russia were the

---

[1]If a work by Dostoevsky other than **The Brothers Karamazov** is referenced, the abbreviated title will appear in the parenthetical citation. Of course, if the text clearly identifies the work as Dostoevsky's, the parenthetical citation will not contain the title.

[2]Luigi Pareyson contends that Dostoevsky saw the contradictions as beginning at the level of God rather than with mankind in general.

> Indeed, in arguing that there is an implicit and inescapable conflict between
> God's justice and his cruelty, Ivan adumbrates for the first time a dialectic with

(continued...)

soul of the planet, the phrase "the Russian Christ" resounds with a special cosmic meaning for Dostoevsky. Smerdyakov, who hates Russia, dreams of leaving Russia and becoming a Frenchman. By contrast, Dmitri exclaims, "I love Russia, Alexei, I love the Russian God, though I myself am a scoundrel" (764; "Epilogue," ch. 2).

For Dostoevsky, a philosopher first and foremost loves to contemplate the eternal question that Russian boys constantly entertain. While in jail, Dmitri refers to the Karamazovs and all "real Russians" as philosophers, not scoundrels, in contrast to Rakitin, who is the soul of expediency and opportunism. Rakitin is not a philosopher despite all his pretensions (588; bk. 11, ch. 4). Dmitri confesses to Alyosha that perhaps he was drinking and fighting and raging because of unknown ideas storming inside him. He was struggling to quell them, confessing, "I'm tormented by God" (592; bk. 11, ch. 4). Dmitri himself, becoming a new man toward the end of the novel, confesses that he had ached for some time to speak to Alyosha and that he had kept silent too long about the eternal question.

> "I've been waiting till this last time to pour out my soul to you. Brother, in these past two months [in prison] I've sensed a new man in me, a new man has arisen in me! He was shut up inside me, but if it weren't for this thunderbolt, he would never have appeared. Frightening! What do I care if I spend twenty years

---

[2](...continued)
> a long tradition behind it--one that is the conclusion of Dostoevsky's meditation: the vision of *conflict within God himself.* (275. Italics added)

Pareyson describes the conflict within God as follows:

> As we meditate on the suffering Christ, we begin to make our way to a dialectic concept of God who has within himself antinomy and contradiction, opposition and contrast, discord and conflict. We grope towards a God who, out of love, is both cruel and merciful towards humans and towards Himself; who, out of love, is cruel towards himself to the point of wanting to suffer, and towards the Son to the point of abandoning Him.... (285)

This theme of discord and conflict within the deity will be explored in Chapter X.

pounding out iron ore in the mines, I'm not afraid of that at all, but I'm afraid of something else now: that this risen man not depart from me!" (591; bk. 11, ch. 4)

Going further to speak of a suffering consciousness and a resurrected hero even in the bowels of the earth, he breaks out with a new view of the world that in some ways resembles Zosima's:

> "And there are many of them [i.e., convicts], there are hundreds, and we're all guilty for them! Why did I have a dream about a 'wee one' at such a moment? 'Why is the wee one poor?' It was a prophecy to me at that moment! It's for the 'wee one' that I will go. Because everyone is guilty for everyone else.... All people are 'wee ones.' And I'll go for all of them, because there must be someone who will go for all of them." (591; bk. 11, ch. 4)

The emerging Dmitri grows pale, and tears pour from his eyes when he exclaims that life is full even underground. "You wouldn't believe, Alexei, how I want to live now, what thirst to exist and be conscious has been born in me precisely within these peeling walls" (592; bk. 11, ch. 4)! He proclaims that because he suffers he exists. He exists because he believes in a world beyond the isolated, atomistic self.

For Karamazovs like Dmitri and Alyosha, no philosophy can exist except through ecstasy. Neither pure subjectivism nor the atom gushing in its own limited walls, ecstasy is the doorway to heaven itself. Through ecstasy, the vision of panentheism or personalism grows stronger and clearer, for the wall separating nature from grace seems artificial. Thus, when Zosima and people like him fall in love with the earth and kiss it, they are in love with God and are kissing the bosom of Mother Earth.

> "Love all of God's creation, both the whole of it and every grain of sand. Love every leaf, every ray of God's light. Love animals, love plants, love each thing. If you love each thing, *you will perceive the mystery of God in things*. Once you have

perceived it, you will begin tirelessly to perceive more and more
of it every day. And you will come at last to love the whole
world with an entire, universal love."
(319; bk. 6, ch. 3 [italics added])

The youngest Karamazov, having inherited the Karamazov intensity for
life, chooses to devote his energy to the image of Christ, thereby following by
choice in the steps of his spiritual father, Zosima. Alyosha, too, wells up with
rapture and ecstasy.

Filled with rapture, his soul yearned for freedom, space,
vastness. Over him the heavenly dome, full of quiet, shining
stars, hung boundlessly. From the zenith to the horizon the
still-dim Milky Way stretched its double strand. Night, fresh
and quiet, almost unstirring, enveloped the earth. The white
towers and golden domes of the church gleamed in the sapphire
sky. The luxuriant autumn flowers in the flowerbeds near the
house had fallen asleep until morning. The silence of the earth
seemed to merge with the silence of the heavens, the mystery of
the earth touched the mystery of the stars.... Alyosha stood
gazing and suddenly, as if he had been cut down, threw himself
to the earth. (362; bk. 7, ch. 4)

This experience of rapture takes place not long after Alyosha has suffered
the despair in knowing that the body of the Elder, far from being supernaturally
preserved in tribute to his saintly reputation, has decomposed prematurely. Having
fallen to the ground in this moment of rapture, he did not know why he was
embracing the earth, and he did not try to comprehend the irresistible urge to kiss
it—all of it—while watering it with his tears. He vowed ecstatically to love it unto
the ages. The words of the Elder rang in his soul: "Water the earth with the tears
of your joy" (362; bk. 7, ch. 4). When he tells of Alyosha's rapture in weeping
for the stars, the narrator unabashedly demonstrates his own ecstasy. He depicts
a swirling vision in which threads of all God's innumerable worlds come together
within Alyosha. Believing that he is "touching other worlds," Alyosha wants to

forgive all for all (362; bk. 7, ch. 4). This clearly marks the turning point in Alyosha's life. The narrator almost sings in his description.

> "He fell to the earth a weak youth and rose up a fighter, steadfast for the rest of his life, and he knew it and felt it suddenly, in that very moment of his ecstasy." (363; bk. 7, ch. 4)

Impossible to exaggerate, the crucial dimension of ecstasy in this most sensitive of the Karamazov men unfolds. Three days after the experience, Alyosha leaves the monastery "to 'sojourn in the world,'" for now he sees the world as touched with teeming life and divinity (363; bk. 7, ch. 4).

Karamazovism is not a reality cut off from humanity in general, but rather a special endowment of all that humans can manifest. In this sense, the Karamazov curse springs not from original guilt, but from almost unbearable responsibility. This means, therefore, that it runs the risk of absurdity and irresponsibility as exemplified in Fyodor Pavlovich.

In some respects, Alyosha, Ivan, and Dmitri inherit Karamazovism through the blood. Otherwise, why does Dostoevsky use the word "Karamazov" as its common thread? On the other hand, Karamazovism serves as a symbol of those special individuals in families both cursed and blessed with this plethoric portion of human nature. Even though Dostoevsky does not explicate the means of the transmission, he appears to have no conscious theory of Lamarckism. Nevertheless, an obscure mixture of Lamarckism and blood transmission of the curse emerges in the novel, which simply does not make clear precisely how the old man's influence and endowment infused themselves into his sons. Ironically, Dostoevsky may have trapped himself in a contradiction. While he apparently rejects Rakitin's theory of the environment as a shaper of the human soul, the novel repeatedly shows that the aspect of the environment controlled by their father had some major influence over their lives. Early in the story, the narrator comments, "Of course, one can imagine what sort of father and mentor such a man would be" (10; bk. 1, ch. 2). Indeed, from Fyodor's mentorship, Dmitri could emulate debauchery and Ivan avarice.

Having acquired by whatever means the blessing and taint of intense passion, the Karamazovs live a life filled with extremes seldom experienced by the majority of families. As Hermann Hesse comments:

> It would not do if there were many such, for the world would go to pieces. This sort of sick man, be he called Dostoevsky or Karamazoff, has that strange occult, godlike faculty, the possibility of which the Asiatic venerates in every maniac. He is a seer and an oracle. A people, a period, a country, a continent has fashioned out of its corpus an organ, a sensory instrument of infinite sensitiveness, a very rare and delicate organ.[1] (44-5)

The Karamazovs, rather than serving as examples of original sin, behave more like sensory instruments of "infinite sensitiveness" through which Dostoevsky can perform laboratory experiments. Dmitri speculates, "Maybe I was drinking and fighting and raging, just because unknown ideas were storming inside me" (592; bk. 11, ch. 4). Almost like a scientist, Dostoevsky seems to use his Karamazovs to test various theories of good and evil.

---

[1]In various works, Dostoevsky uses the motif of "the holy fool" as something of a noble experiment by which to test extraordinary dimensions of human existence. The novel *The Idiot* is his principal experiment. See First Corinthians 3:18 and 4:10 for the Apostle Paul's reference to the fool for Christ sake.

Chapter IV. Original Conflict:
A Broader View of Sin

In *The Brothers Karamazov*, if paradise lies in acceptance, forgiveness, and love in all their interrelationships, hell abides in a life drained of love or left to its own base devices. And hell resides in the human race at war with itself inwardly and outwardly. But do humans enter life in a state of hell or at least in a state of depravity and baseness? *The Brothers Karamazov* appears to have a doctrine of original evil irreducible to any major theological doctrine preceding it.

Of course, Dostoevsky did not create his concept of original evil *ex nihilo*, for it has deep roots in Christian theology, going back at least to the major contenders in the battle over original sin, that is, to Augustine and Pelagius. Neither agreeing with Pelagius that an infant enters the world as a wholly harmless creature nor agreeing with Augustine that the infant is sinful, *The Brothers Karamazov* advances another view that grew out of the controversy and soared

beyond it. The marks of both Pelagius and Augustine nevertheless show on the face of this novel.

A Russian work through and through, the novel also displays the view of the Eastern Church, which has other sources in addition to its deep roots in both Pelagius and Augustine. As an advocate of the Russian Orthodox Church, Dostoevsky objected to the West's decision-making process. In the Roman Catholic Church, the pope made many of the important decisions unilaterally, despite his emotional and physical distance from the people. Less than a decade before *The Brothers Karamazov* began to appear in print, Pope Pius IX succeeded in having the papal office declared infallible when its occupants spoke *ex cathedra* (Hasler 81). Under Protestantism, various forms of church government flourished, ranging from episcopal authority to congregational democracy. In the Russian Orthodox Church, on the other hand, a consensus of the people was sought (Gibson 42). Dostoevsky admired the Russian Orthodox Church's ability to forego authoritarian absolutes and to cope with contradictions. A. Boyce Gibson states that Dostoevsky's years of living in Europe made him even more devoutly Russian Orthodox. Dostoevsky objected to the moral and social absolutes and the compartmentalism in Europe. "He developed almost a fixation on the *Vsechelovek*, the 'all-man', who can encompass the whole of human experience, discrepancies included" (33).

Given its capacity to cope with contradictions, the Eastern Church never nailed down a fixed doctrine of original sin. Instead, in this branch of christendom, the idea of original sin floats between the extremes of total depravity and pristine free will.

The Brothers Karamazov spawns the doctrine of "original conflict" to replace the Augustinian version of original sin and guilt. At birth, human beings come into a thoroughly social world. Human mortals must relate to one another. The very idea of a self-contained individual forms an abstraction that represents no reality. A Russian thinker like Dostoevsky would find atomistic individualism completely foreign. "He found it [individualism]

simple-minded to the point of being infantile..." (Gibson 28). Nicholas Berdyaev interprets Dostoevsky on this issue as follows:

> Unrestrained and objectless freedom...ceases to be capable of making a choice and is bandied about in opposite directions. Then is the time that two selves appear in a man and his personality is cloven apart. (109)

Dostoevsky illustrates the cloven personality bandied in opposite directions in the characters of Dmitri and Ivan. A paradox of opposing physical appearances, emotions, behaviors, and ideas, Dmitri epitomizes Dostoevsky's concept of unrestrained and objectless freedom, at least until Dmitri's salvation. While his muscular body and his sudden, frenetic actions make him seem young, his sunken cheeks and ashen coloring make him look sickly and "much older than his years".[1] More than any of his other features, his dark eyes exhibit contradictions. Simultaneously conveying determination and ambiguity, his large eyes look pensive even when he laughs[2] his clipped, wooden laugh.[3] Though Dmitri conducts his life in a wild and disorderly fashion, he dresses impeccably; and, despite the fact that he has a moustache, he keeps his beard shaved and his dark brown hair cut short.[4] A recently retired lieutenant, he has a long, resolute military stride;[5] yet, we see him "wildly gesticulating, waving and beckoning" or "'whispering like a fool when there is no need to'".[6]

Emotional and behavioral incongruities abound in Dmitri. Calling himself a depraved lover of cruelty and an evil insect, Dmitri also describes himself as honorable.[7] Others say he has a stormy soul; and, though meek and honest, he

---

[1](67; bk. 2, ch. 6)

[2](67-8; bk. 2, ch. 6)

[3](372; bk. 8, ch. 1)

[4](67-8; bk. 2, ch. 6)

[5](67-8; bk. 2, ch. 6)

[6](103; bk. 3, ch. 3)

[7](109; bk. 3, ch. 4)

will as a sensualist in a fit of passion kill for the love of a woman's body.[1] Madman,[2] scoundrel,[3] viper,[4] earthy and violent,[5] disorderly and absurd[6]—vile epithets frequently thrown at him—counter positive ones like trustful and noble,[7] gentle and meek,[8] tender,[9] good-hearted and grateful,[10] light-minded,[11] and sensitive.[12]

Likewise, the novel portrays Ivan as a cloven personality whose heavy flirtations with egoistic freedom lead to madness. The novel depicts Ivan as having two personalities. First, during a large portion of the story, Ivan seems intellectual, not emotional and intuitive, and consistent, not erratic.[13] Ivan seems to have "an unusual and brilliant aptitude for learning",[14] has obtained a degree in natural science from the university, and has published newspaper articles and book reviews.[15] Known for his curious and quaint writing and his cold common sense, Ivan never loses his contacts with editors, and he frequents literary circles.[16] Ivan rejects substances and circumstances that might induce irrational

---

[1](79; bk. 2, ch. 7)

[2](139; bk. 3, ch. 9)

[3](153; bk. 3, ch. 11)

[4](187; bk. 4, ch. 5)

[5](220; bk. 5, ch. 1)

[6](432; bk. 8, ch. 8)

[7](381; bk. 8, ch. 3)

[8](396; bk. 8, ch. 5)

[9](508; bk. 9, ch. 9)

[10](673; bk. 12, ch. 3)

[11](732; bk. 12, ch. 11)

[12](742; bk. 12, ch. 13)

[13](228; bk. 5, ch. 3)

[14](15; bk. 1, ch. 3)

[15](16; bk. 1, ch. 3)

[16](16; bk. 1, ch. 3)

behavior; he dislikes drinking and debauchery.[1] Furthermore, Victor Terras hears in Ivan a fake, shifting voice, one that lacks poetry (***Companion*** 90-2).

Nevertheless, the novel sometimes reveals an Ivan of an opposite personality and nature. Fyodor accuses him of overstating his level of education and of having more of an interest in money than he admits.[2] In fact, Ivan sometimes seems less the rational intellectual than he does the passionate, irrational Karamazov, given to flashes of insight and sudden inexplicable convictions. For example, knowing full well the identity of the murderer, Ivan suddenly decides that he will tell the prosecutor the truth. Relieved of his tormenting doubts, he immediately feels "a sort of joy...[descend] into his soul".[3] Just as suddenly, all his resolve melts, dissolving his newly found joy and self-content.[4] Ivan's attempts to live his maxim that "everything is permitted," his attempt to exercise limitless freedom, has led to his madness.[5]

In other words, no human can exert his or her own free will limitlessly. Inevitably, one person's will collides with another. Each must then make choices that consider the other or else face disintegration into madness, a state known more for its lack of control than for its self-will.

Those who fail to restrain self-centeredness and pride in particular will lose the capacity to love. For Dostoevsky, love involves people interacting; otherwise, people relate to useless ideals, which "easily become a high-minded imaginative substitute for action. They [ideals] split the will from the deed"

---

[1] (17; bk. 1, ch. 3)

[2] (173; bk. 4, ch. 2)

[3] (633; bk. 11, ch. 8)

[4] (634; bk. 11, ch. 8)

[5] Gary Saul Morson contends that Smerdyakov sets up a double bind that drives "Ivan Karamazov mad by repeated interpretations, and interpretations of previous interpretations, of a coded conversation" (93). Faced with the contradictions in his philosophy and in his behavior, Ivan loses his sanity. Yet, Aileen Kelly contends that Dostoevsky himself saw that belief systems could not escape contradictions. According to Kelly, the following represents the Russian radical intelligentsia's interpretation of Dostoevsky between 1905 and 1917:

> To be internally consistent...ethical systems (and the religious and political creeds that embodied them) must...ignore or deny some of the moral imperatives rooted in man's nature. No system of belief, however compelling, could thus confer immunity from guilt, doubt, or self-contempt. (239)

(Gibson 17). In a letter to his brother Michael, Dostoevsky confessed, "I could give my life for you and yours; but even when my heart is warm with love, people often can't get so much as one friendly word out of me" ("To His Brother" 44).

For Dostoevsky, free will can never mean a limitless will floating free of all human contexts. If Dostoevsky's novels exhibit human freedom par excellence, his image of freedom always reveals human beings exerting themselves in relationships with each other. Freedom cannot conceivably exist for a solipsist. For freedom to exist, it must always occur in connections. At that point, however, sin enters through the doorway.

The Brothers Karamazov presupposes that human life begins in conflict. Why? Humans have limited perception and understanding. An intimate connection between ignorance and sin exists, not as an instance of evil, but as a precondition. This point deserves development.

Human beings come into the world with a propensity to express themselves, to satisfy themselves, and to cultivate passion and commitment. As creatures of desire, they long for teleological fulfillment, reaching beyond themselves into the world of nature and human society. They even desire new desires. Given not only the ignorance of human beings, but their desire for objects in a common world and their propensity for passion and commitment, conflict inevitably arises.

If human creatures enjoyed omniscience, they would foresee all the consequences of their actions and could conceivably avoid all clashes. For Dostoevsky, however, the dream of omniscience manifests pride, itself born of ignorance. Even Ivan sees the absurdity of the dream of scientific omniscience emerging from the earthly Euclidean mind. Doomed to a continual state of partial knowledge and considerable ignorance, humans cannot avoid conflict.

In *The Brothers Karamazov*, when the motif of paradise on earth arises, it does not project a society of passionless harmony. Without passion, both life and meaning perish. Conflict inevitably appears where passion and desire dwell. By claiming to be in paradise *now*, Zosima's older brother does not mean a state of sinless perfection. If the birds do not sin, it is because they cannot sin and because God did not make them in his image and likeness in the exalted sense in which he made human beings. By this earthly paradise, Zosima's brother means a state of mutual forgiveness. "Let me be sinful before everyone, but so that everyone will forgive me, and that is paradise. Am I not in paradise now?"

(290; bk. 6, ch. 2) Just before proclaiming to his mama that he is in paradise, he describes this state in which each bears guilt and recognizes such guilt. The absence of sin does not make it paradise. Instead, paradise comes from the presence of forgiveness and the joy and peace that accompany the forgiveness process: repentance, perspective about oneself, and the unwillingness to hold a grudge. Did not Zosima himself as a young man understand this when, instead of taking his rightful shot at the man who had challenged him to a duel, he threw away the gun and at the same moment threw revenge to the wind? (299-300; bk. 6, ch. 2)

Born into a state of contradictions, each individual must at every moment face the fork in the road: one direction leading to humility; the other to inordinate pride. Pride comes in many forms just because the individual must make decisions regarding himself or herself in relation to others.

First, pride derives from ignorance that leads a person to perceive himself or herself mistakenly as more righteous than others. Over and over, the Elder Zosima tells the monks that they sin more than those outside the monastery.

> "For we are not holier than those in the world because we have come here and shut ourselves within these walls, but, on the contrary, anyone who comes here, by the very fact that he has come, already knows himself to be worse than all those who are in the world, worse than all on earth.... And the longer a monk lives within his walls, the more keenly he must be aware of it. For otherwise he had no reason to come here."
> (163-4; bk. 4, ch. 1)

Zosima tells this to the monks, not simply to cultivate humility in the monastery, but to make them face an essential truth.

Pride develops in another way when, after incorrectly perceiving their own moral status in the world, individuals set out to demand recognition of their superiority. Soon this demand leads to requiring subservience and treating others as instruments of one's own self importance. A subtle demonstration occurs in the brilliant scene in which Katerina and Grushenka, with Alyosha listening, seek through the guise of humility to establish dominance one over the other (150; bk. 3, ch. 10). A dramatic instance, basic to the plot, happens when Dmitri bows to Katerina after he has tricked her into offering herself to him

(114; bk. 3, ch. 4). Her humiliation entices her to attempt in several ways to humiliate him in return.

With devastating irony, Dostoevsky shows that humility can become the slave of pride. Filled with pride in his meticulous performance of ascetic gamesmanship, Father Ferapont in the monastery not only mistakenly perceives himself but "sees" a demon sitting on the chest of a rival monk (335; bk. 7, ch. 1). This, of course, allows Father Ferapont to demote his rival and to elevate himself.

In *The Idiot*, Dostoevsky writes about a good man embodying humility in the world of conflict and pride. In the end, the good man not only suffers but is ground up. In *The Brothers Karamazov*, Dostoevsky experiments again with a good man in the world. Through Father Zosima, Dostoevsky suggests that monks like Alyosha should go out into the world beyond the monastery to generate active love.

Alyosha, the author's hero, exemplifies the good man. People enjoy this humble man's companionship. Never judging them as his inferiors, he avoids injuring their pride. Edward Wasiolek interprets Dostoevsky as saying that the beast within us causes us to exert our self-will and to use it to inflict pain on others even when we initially intended to show them love. Alyosha's teacher demonstrates that the only way to overcome this human foible is to accept everyone no matter how corrupt he or she may appear. Only by considering himself more sinful than others, however, does Zosima discover the key to unlocking his total acceptance of others. Until then, Zosima carried with him the taint of a self-perceived superiority.

After the Elder Zosima decomposes, Alyosha wallows for a brief period in self-pity over the humiliation of his hero and thus over his own hurt pride. It takes a fellow sinner, one whom most people would consider capable of vicious spite, to save Alyosha from his rebellion. By telling a moving story of a woman in hell who by a deed of selfishness lost her chance to escape to heaven, Grushenka facilitates Alyosha's dreaming of Christ's miracles of turning the water into wine at the marriage in Cana. He awakens free of his self-pity and full of joy for the happiness of others (Wasiolek 177-9).

The narrator insists, however, that the realist Alyosha believes in miracles because he first had faith, not that he acquired faith because he experienced miracles (25; bk. 1, ch. 5). The narrator calls Alyosha a realist, partly for his

phenomenal acceptance of himself and his place in the community. Unlike Ivan, Alyosha does not resent his dependency upon others. At the same time, he knows little of subservience. Even when his father attempts to dominate him, telling him to leave the monastery, for example, Alyosha good-naturedly ignores the command. On the other hand, he has taken an oath of obedience to another father, the Elder; and he childishly elevates the Elder above human stature. Nevertheless, even here Dostoevsky portrays Alyosha as a youth in the process of outgrowing this aspect of subservience.

In some ways, the Elder serves young Alyosha, for Alyosha voluntarily went to the monastery to gain—under the Elder's guidance—greater freedom from the pursuit of self-will (27-8; bk. 1, ch. 5). Alyosha uses the Elder as his spiritual guide. Quite aware of the dynamics of their relationship, Zosima accepts it as mutually beneficial. The Elder fulfills gladly the role as a spiritual coach and takes delight in the progress of his trainee.

Already Zosima sees Alyosha as in some ways more advanced than himself and ready to face the world. Whereas the Elder must wait for the world to come to him to receive his blessing and counsel, Alyosha lives and interacts in the outer world of conflict on his mission to mingle with fellow sinners and to sow the seed of love and sacrifice wherever he goes. Indeed, as the mediator, Alyosha repeatedly stands between the opposing parties in the hotbed of devastating conflict.

By contrast, Ivan often takes refuge in his private cave, his Euclidean mind. While not a monastery, Ivan's private world of thoughts and ideas partially insulates him from the conflicts that human relationships would naturally bring. Dmitri tells Alyosha, "Ivan knows everything. He's known it for a long time before you. But Ivan is a grave" (110; bk. 3, ch. 4). Yet, portrayed as a man ambivalent about living in this world, even Ivan dearly loves Alyosha and says that a god in the image of Alyosha would be a worthy deity. This again demonstrates that Alyosha not only mediates amid conflict and treachery, but inspires more love.

While Ivan attempts to escape conflict by withdrawing into his passionless intellect, Dmitri falls so fervently into the passion of sensuality that he deprives himself of other avenues of passion. Intellectually a dwarf, emotionally a cripple, and morally an adolescent on the way toward adulthood, Dmitri recognizes the immaturity and dangerous nature of the force of love in him. He knows that his state of being in love seldom results in loving behavior on his part. In fact, his form of love increases the conflict among the characters in the novel.

Linked to Dostoevsky's doctrine of original conflict is the thesis that paradise on earth develops only when people actively forgive one another. The existence of forgiveness in the world presupposes unavoidable and inevitable conflict. And where conflict exists, according to the whole drift of *The Brothers Karamazov*, sin and moral evil inevitably occur.

With Pelagius, Dostoevsky seems to say that the individual starts life free of sin and guilt. Dostoevsky even depicts some youths as neither evil nor wicked even when they behave wickedly. In one of Father Zosima's recollections of his youthful years, he tells of the pride he and his fellow officers had in their drunken boasting. Yet, Zosima says, "I would not say we were wicked; they were all good young men, but they behaved wickedly, and I most of all" (296; bk. 6, ch. 2).

With Augustine, on the other hand, Dostoevsky does see the inevitability of sin as a part of the human condition. Upon interacting with others, the newborn human eventually will step on the first rung of the ladder of sin; and, in the words of Alyosha, "Whoever steps on the lowest step will surely step on the highest" (109; bk. 3, ch. 4).

According to Zosima and his brother, in paradise on earth we experience not the ultimate resolution of all conflict, but rather conflict, inevitable moral evil, and forgiveness. Apparently, on earth people can live the life of humility, but not a life absent of sin or of conflict. Indeed, in some ways, for Dostoevsky, the elevation of the species to higher consciousness, forgiveness, and love presupposes, as F. R. Tennant suggests, the prior fall of the species on earth (105-11).

The question as to why conflict must exist at all raises images of a world devoid of freedom. Only if some omniscient being totally predetermined and controlled human behavior could a conflict-free world emerge. Consequently, *The Brothers Karamazov* proceeds on the presupposition that only where no human life abides can the possibility of sinlessness surface. But with human life emerges consciousness, freedom, and therefore sinfulness.

Chapter V. Freedom, Suffering, and Love: The Fruit of Original Conflict

Father Zosima pictures the world, apart from human beings, as sinless. Animals cannot commit moral evil.

> "Gentlemen," I cried suddenly from the bottom of my heart, "look at the divine gifts around us: the clear sky, the fresh air, the tender grass, the birds, nature is beautiful and sinless, and

we, we alone, are godless and foolish, and do not understand
that life is paradise, for we need only wish to understand, and it
will come at once in all its beauty, and we shall embrace each
other and weep...." (299; bk. 6, ch. 2)

Animal paradise lacks sin apparently because no animal can experience
the self-consciousness that leads to grossly mistaken perceptions of oneself and
others, perceptions that lead to pride and its malicious progeny. Only humans
reflect the image and likeness of God, at least in one crucial respect: they have
freedom born of intense consciousness (298-9; bk. 6, ch. 2). But this freedom
opens the door to status anxiety, vanity, pride, shame, rage, treachery, and
murder.

Although Dostoevsky in *The Brothers Karamazov* gives voice to a
doctrine of kinship between human beings and other species, he differs somewhat
from Darwin on the nature of the kinship. Dostoevsky wrestled all of his adult life
with the question of determinism and the extent to which human actions are caused
by their biological inheritance, their environment, and other conditioning
processes. It is as if he had anticipated his fellow Russian Ivan Petrovich Pavlov,
who only two decades after Dostoevsky's death refined what is today called
classical conditioning. According to F. F. Seely, Dostoevsky objected strongly to
psychological determinism, which blames social deviancy upon the environment
(121). During Dmitri's trial, he disparagingly refers to Rakitin as a Bernard,
implying Claude Bernard, a nineteenth-century French physiologist whose
positivism included sociocultural determinism.

> Infuriated by the tone in which Rakitin referred to Grushenka,
> he [Dmitri] suddenly cried out from his place: "Bernard!" And
> when, after all the questioning of Rakitin was over, the presiding
> judge addressed the defendant, asking him if he had any
> observations to make, Mitya shouted in a booming voice:
>
> "He kept hitting me for loans, even in prison! A
> despicable Bernard and careerist, and he doesn't believe in God,
> he hoodwinked His Grace!" (668; bk. 12, ch. 2)

In contrast to Bernard's view, *The Brothers Karamazov* paints a picture of the human world as not only influenced by inherited traits, but molded by conflict and free choice.

According to Darwin, original conflict began before the arrival of homo sapiens. Even though he did not treat this original conflict in a strictly theological context, he did apparently understand that it had moral implications for at least one of the primates. For Dostoevsky, conflict among animals does not raise the question of sin, perhaps because non-human animals lack the special consciousness that allows them to judge others and themselves morally in terms of rank and status.

Interestingly, the eighteenth-century French social theorist and philosopher Jean Jacques Rousseau theorized that corruption did not arise in humans until they had evolved consciousness and intelligence enough to rely more on one another for survival than on their own brute strength as individuals.

> As ideas and feelings succeeded one another, and heart and head were brought into play, men continued to lay aside their original wildness; their private connections became every day more intimate as their limits extended. They accustomed themselves to assemble before their huts around a large tree; singing and dancing, the true offspring of love and leisure, became the amusement, or rather the occupation, of men and women thus assembled together with nothing else to do. Each one began to consider the rest, and to wish to be considered in turn; and thus a value came to be attached to public esteem. Whoever sang or danced best, whoever was the handsomest, the strongest, the most dexterous, or the most eloquent, came to be of most consideration; and this was the first step toward inequality, and at the same time towards vice. From these first distinctions arose on the one side vanity and contempt and on the other shame and envy: and the fermentation caused by these new leavens ended by producing combinations fatal to innocence and happiness. (241-2)

Beliefs and ideas also cause friction among humans. For Dostoevsky, human individuals carry beliefs with them as a kind of mirror in which to examine perpetually the self and others. Stated even more strongly, human individuals seem capable of being carried by their beliefs, whereas other species have no such ability. Undoubtedly, *The Brothers Karamazov* is a novel of ideas and beliefs and the impact they make on the lives of individuals in the story. Ideas have consequences within the tale. For the human species, the conflict increases because the ideas to which individuals adhere come into conflict and make a kind of creative war on each other.

The Brothers Karamazov, a polyphonic novel, overflows with rival beliefs playing off one another. According to Mikhail Bakhtin, *"The plurality of independent and unmerged voices and consciousnesses and the genuine polyphony of full-valued voices are in fact characteristics of Dostoevsky's novels"* (4).

Professor Victor Terras offers examples of the way *The Brothers Karamazov* makes a series of points and counterpoints.

> Once "The Grand Inquisitor" has been read, responses to it can be recognized frequently throughout the rest of the novel. Father Zosima's wisdom contains some responses to it.... The entire episode of "An Odor of Corruption" is a counterpoint to the theme of the second temptation of Christ. Aliosha's vision in "Cana of Galilee" is the counterpoint to Ivan's later "vision" of the devil, and thus a response to "The Grand Inquisitor" as well. Grushen'ka's folk tale, "The Onion," echoes Ivan's paraphrase of "The Virgin's Descent to Hell." It emphasizes the belief that everybody can be saved—provided he wants to be saved. (*Companion* 105-6)

The supreme point-counterpoint of the novel occurs in the conflict between the belief system of Ivan and that of Zosima. In one way or another, starting at the level of psychology and carried to the heights of theodicy, the question of what to do with conflict dominates the entire novel.

Ivan provides the chilling example of human life in its blazing self-consciousness. He challenges heaven itself, demanding that the deity, if such

exists, justify his world. In "The Grand Inquisitor," Ivan's position gains representation by another old man, the Inquisitor himself, a more ancient man than the Elder. The question arises as to whether he is also wiser than Zosima. The Inquisitor contends that Christ expects too much of his human creatures, that he throws them in effect into more conflict than they can handle.

Ironically, whereas Zosima supposedly said that most people need looking after like children, the Inquisitor develops a plan for putting this belief into practice. Alyosha says, "You know, Lise, my elder said once that most people need to be looked after like children, and some like the sick in hospitals..." (217; bk. 5, ch. 1). In Ivan's "The Grand Inquisitor," the aged cardinal says to Christ:

> "Oh, we shall finally convince them not to be proud, for you
> raised them up and thereby taught them pride; we shall prove to
> them that they are feeble, that they are only pitiful children....
> Oh, we will allow them to sin, too; they are weak and
> powerless, and they will love us like children for allowing them
> to sin." (259; bk. 5, ch. 5)

With double irony, Dostoevsky represents both Zosima and the Inquisitor as saying that *most* people should be treated like children. The Inquisitor charges Christ with advancing a religion for only the elect, a spiritual elite, and with, in effect, forgetting the weak. The irony cuts still deeper, and the Inquisitor sees it clearly when he accuses Christ of generating pride in the elite-elect. In one of the most shocking speeches in the entire novel, Ivan charges that the conflicts and the absurdities of life are too much. He makes his point with such telling brilliance that it becomes clear that no eventual earthly harmony could ever justify God's creation of his favored species. Since Dostoevsky aligns with Zosima and Alyosha rather than with the Inquisitor and Ivan, only one avenue opens for Dostoevsky to answer Ivan's challenge. The existence of the horrendous conflict on earth demands that life go on beyond this Euclidean point. Immortality, for Zosima, must exist, for "only the idea of immortality stands between tears and despair, suffering and rebellion" (Jackson 321). Only if time touches eternity can there be the order and the harmony that earthly conflict seems to demand. Without immortality, there is no meaning. Without the conflict, on the other hand,

Dostoevsky seems to imply, no truly human life, and therefore no meaning worthy of the human species, can exist.

Dmitri in many ways exemplifies the life of human conflict. Conflict, so obvious in the eldest son, begins in a fight with his father, with whom he battles over money and the same woman. Dmitri even finds conflict in love, on the one hand loving Katerina and on the other hand loving Grushenka. If he has in his father a rival for Grushenka, he has in Ivan a rival for Katerina. Even the normally insightful Alyosha puzzles over the object of Dmitri's love. He sees the conflict but cannot determine which of the two women Dmitri truly loves. The conflict compounds when Dmitri comes to see that he has two kinds of love in him that conflict with one another.

Everywhere he turns he meets conflict. A man of generous heart, Dmitri humiliates the bearded captain in front of others because of a quarrel over money. Katerina Ivanovna tells Alyosha about Dmitri's depraved behavior.

> "A week ago—yes, a week, I think—Dmitri Fyodorovich committed a rash and unjust act, a very ugly act. There is a bad place here, a tavern. In it he met that retired officer, that captain, whom your father employed in some business of his. Dmitri Fyodorovich got very angry with this captain for some reason, seized him by the beard in front of everyone, led him outside in that humiliating position, and led him a long way down the street, and they say that the boy, the captain's son, who goes to the local school, just a child, saw it and went running along beside them, crying loudly and begging for his father, and rushing up to everyone asking them to defend him, but everyone laughed. (193; bk. 4, ch. 5)

With blood on his hands, face, and clothing, Dmitri carelessly presents himself in public and recklessly spends large sums of money on food and wine to impress Grushenka (399; bk. 8., ch. 5). Then he rashly breaks in on Grushenka and her young officer's party.

> "Gentlemen," he began loudly, almost shouting, but stammering at each word, "it's...it's nothing! Don't be afraid,"

he exclaimed, "it's really nothing, nothing," he suddenly turned to Grushenka, who was leaning towards Kalganov in her armchair, firmly clutching his hand. "I...I am traveling, too. I'll stay till morning." (416; bk. 8, ch. 7)

Alyosha, the most tranquil of the brothers, nevertheless has his own war. A careful reading of the novel suggests that Alyosha is being prepared for a series of battles. Within the novel, he recognizes his own personal conflict and believes that he went initially to the monastery to find a way to deal with it. On the one hand, he is the son of a profligate. On the other hand, he is stirred by the memory of his mother as she holds him before the icon.

> He [Alyosha] remembered a quiet summer evening, an open window, the slanting rays of the setting sun (these slanting rays he remembered most of all), an icon in the corner of the room, a lighted oil-lamp in front of it, and before the icon, on her knees, his mother, sobbing as if in hysterics, with shrieks and cries, seizing him in her arms, hugging him so tightly that it hurt, and pleading for him to the Mother of God, holding him out from her embrace with both arms towards the icon, as if under the protection of the Mother of God...and suddenly a nurse rushes in and snatches him from her in fear. (18-9; bk. 1, ch. 4)

Later, the narrator reveals that Alyosha may have grown fond of the monastery because of memories of his mother's having taken him there for Sunday liturgy. The narrator speculates:

> Perhaps he was also affected by the slanting rays of the setting sun before the icon to which his mother, the "shrieker," held him out. Thoughtful, he came to us, then, maybe only to see if it was "all" here, or if here, too, there were only "two roubles." (27; bk. 1, ch. 5)

On the surface, suffering seems to play a mysterious part in *The Brothers Karamazov*. Suffering might even look like an end in itself, a masochistic orgy Russian style. Indeed, Zosima implies that suffering and happiness are somehow linked, although the nature of the link lies in obscurity. Only a thorough understanding of Dostoevsky's doctrine of original conflict can make sense out of the prevalence of suffering in the novel.

At least two major sources of suffering emerge. Above all, suffering comes naturally as a normal part of finite human existence in conflict. To live is to risk suffering. Given human ignorance and its contingencies, as well as family life and other social matrices, suffering inevitably occurs. Dostoevsky does not make an abstract moral principle of suffering or urge his readers to suffer,[1] but rather he avers that one can escape all suffering only by bowing out and leaving the stage of life. Even Ivan, who seems to suffer intensely, cannot imagine dashing the cup until he is thirty. It is crucial to understand that *The Brothers Karamazov* is a theodicy, that is, an attempt to give some wider meaning to suffering. In part, the meaning lies in the fact that suffering occurs simply as a byproduct of living. Its connection with life in all its fullness *is* its meaning.

---

[1]Found guilty by the "jury of peasants," who lacked "imagination, empathy, and inspiration" (Terras, "Art" 202), Dmitri, a man with "intuition, empathy, and imagination" will suffer unjustly (Terras, "Art" 198). But Dostoevsky then has Alyosha tell Dmitri:

> "Listen, then: you're not ready, and such a cross is not for you. Moreover, unready as you are, you don't need such a great martyr's cross. If you had killed your father, I would regret that you rejected your cross. But you're innocent, and such a cross is too much for you. You wanted to regenerate another man in yourself through suffering; I say just remember that other man always, all your life, and wherever you escape to—and that is enough for you. That you did not accept that great cross will only serve to make you feel a still greater duty in yourself, and through this constant feeling from now on, all your life, you will do more for your generation, perhaps, than if you went *there* [Siberia]. Because there you will not endure, you will begin to murmur, and in the end you may really say: 'I am quits.' The attorney was right about that. Heavy burdens are not for everyone, for some they are impossible." (763-4; epilogue, ch. 2)

Why should life and suffering be linked? That is the burning question demanding an answer in any theodicy worthy of the name. Does Dostoevsky deal with it forthrightly? Unlike John Milton, he does not draw on a pre-earthly existence, when God and Satan set the stage for the emergence of evil, pain, and suffering. In fact, Dostoevsky allows the Elder to recall the criticisms raised against one of the biblical ventures into theodicy:

> "And so much in it [i.e., the story of Job] is great, mysterious, inconceivable! Later I heard the words of the scoffers and blasphemers, proud words: how could the Lord hand over the most beloved of his saints for Satan to play with him, to take away his children, to smite him with disease and sores so that he scraped the pus from his wounds with a potsherd, and all for what? Only so as to boast before Satan: 'See what my saint can suffer for my sake!'" (292; bk. 6, ch. 2)

Dostoevsky knows full well that he has entered into the heights of theodicy and that he cannot offer point for point refutations of Voltaire and other critics of classical theism.

A second source and kind of suffering, *nadryv*, only an honest genius like Dostoevsky would dare expose, even if it sends another arrow into the heart of his theodicy. The Richard Pevear and Larissa Volokhonsky translation of the novel uses "laceration" as a translation of *nadryv*. Masochists embrace laceration—Lise slamming the door on her finger deliberately, for example. The word "laceration" or "eruption" occurs again and again throughout the novel, and it almost always contains the element of self-injury or self-punishment.

Professor Victor Terras explains that *nadryv* develops for several characters in the novel when they fail to live up to the image they have of themselves and that they desire others to have of them. Terras defines *nadryv* as a strain or a rupture; and he indicates that it happens to Lise, Katerina, Ivan, and Snegiryov (*Companion* 82).

Edward Wasiolek summarizes examples of laceration in the novel as follows:

Father Ferapont's ascetic deprivations are a self-denial from *nadryv*. He "hurts" himself, so that he can hurt the other monks; he needs the "indulgent" monks (which his exercises in asceticism create) as much as Katerina needs a fallen Dmitry. Father Ferapont's ascetic deprivations are weapons of humiliation of others and exaltation of self....

Katerina *loves* from *nadryv*; Father Ferapont *fasts* from *nadryv*; Captain Snegirev *loves honor* from *nadryv*....

Ivan has his *nadryv* also, for his hurt is his bruised sense of justice. (160)

Keeping in mind that Dostoevsky antedates Freud, one need not conjecture that Dostoevsky has developed a systematic theory of laceration. He does nevertheless provide an adequate framework to make possible an interpretation of this strange phenomenon. Indeed, Dostoevsky seems to see self-injury as not strange after all to the creature created in the image of God. It is peculiar to that species. Why? The answer appears to lie in the fact that conflict and consciousness form so much a part of human life that the individual in some ways represents a kind of society at war with itself. Early in his literary career, Dostoevsky wrote a novella entitled **The Double,** which portrays a man over against himself. Self-injury, self-laceration, is perhaps one dimension of the self electing to punish another dimension.

Chapter VI. Inevitable Suffering and the Unifying Power of Love

Dostoevsky's theodicy struggles with the question of universal harmony or the ultimate resolution of all conflicts. Ivan protests not against harmony per se—indeed, he has his own version of unity on earth—but against certain ingredients that go into unity. He protests in particular against the suffering of innocent children and demands to know what could possibly justify their torment. Through Father Zosima, Dostoevsky advances the thesis that harmony exists at various levels and that only the higher harmony, which includes both this Euclidean earth and eternity, is worthy of God. Better a life of suffering and conflict when it leads to the higher values than the life of the anthill, where presumably the anguish and horror experienced by human mortals never emerge. This radical doctrine implies that the quality of a world that includes human sin exceeds that of a Garden in which Adam and Eve roam in pristine innocence. Dostoevsky comes close to suggesting that God could not have created his best world without also creating freedom and all the terrible risks that follow in the train of freedom.

Zosima's version of redemption introduces a special kind of suffering, which goes beyond mere masochism and must above all never be confused with masochism. If, as the Elder believes, all people so intricately impact the lives of others that when one sins all sin, then it follows invariably that when one suffers all suffer.

> "My young brother asked forgiveness of the birds: it seems senseless, yet it is right, for all is like an ocean, all flows and connects; touch it in one place and it echoes at the other end of the world.... All is like an ocean, I say to you. Tormented by universal love, you, too, would then start praying to the birds, as if in a sort of ecstasy, and entreat them to forgive you your sin. Cherish this ecstasy, however senseless it may seem to people." (319-20; bk. 6, ch. 3)[1]

Zosima goes further to say that not only Christ, but the whole body of Christ, indeed the whole of humanity, bears the torment and suffering of sin. He urges his fellow monks to give up the desire to revenge themselves upon the wicked.

> "Go at once and seek torments for yourself, as if you yourself were guilty of their wickedness. Take those torments upon yourself and suffer them, and your heart will be eased, and you will understand that you, too, are guilty...." (321; bk. 6, ch. 3)

---

[1]In his book about the structure of *The Brothers Karamazov*, Robert Belknap includes some interesting diagrams that show the changes in the relationships in the novel that occur because Alyosha leaves the monastery and enters the outside world. Belknap first draws a hexagon to depict the relationships of the characters in the early part of the novel. The hexagon connects Grushenka to Alyosha, Alyosha to Lise, Lise to Ivan, Ivan to Katerina, Katerina to Dmitri, Dmitri to Grushenka, and Grushenka to the Pole. In short, each person's love goes unrequited. To graph the relationships that develop after Alyosha leaves the monastery, however, Belknap uses six parallel lines, showing mutual love between Grushenka and Dmitri, between Alyosha and Lise, and between Ivan and Katerina (*Structure* 70). In the eyes of Belknap, evidently each person does have a rippling effect upon the human community.

The emphasis is on the oneness of the human race.

Readers from the West will perhaps stumble over the passages in which Zosima, Alyosha, and others kiss the earth and water it with their tears. This strange and spontaneous practice, however, manifests the feeling of oneness, not an excessive sentimentality. Even as God sends rain for the just and unjust alike, so the believer waters the earth and pours forth his heart for everyone without discrimination. The practice manifests also rapture and ecstasy in which apparently the believer can participate in the higher oneness or harmony. If this properly interprets Zosima, one has the key to understanding the passages in which Dostoevsky's believers pray for the forgiveness of not only their own sins but also the sins of others. Human beings may even dare to ask forgiveness on behalf of each other because they are so intricately bound to one another.

Love and Unity on Earth

1 ——▶	2 ——▶	3 ——▶	4 ——▶
Life as Desire and Passion	Original Conflict (intraconflict and interconflict)	Inevitable Suffering	Consciousness and Misperception Regarding Self and Others

5 ——▶	6 ——▶	7 ——▶	8 ——▶
Inevitable Status Anxiety and Sin (Pride, Rebellion, and Arrogance)	Deep Suffering and Perverse Suffering	Guilt	Forgiveness and Redemptive Suffering

The diagram summarizes Dostoevsky's schema whereby unifying love and redemption necessarily include original conflict. The supreme values incorporated in forgiveness and redemptive suffering on earth (No. 8 on the diagram) are abstractions if they are without desire and passion (No. 1) and are without all the other ingredients (Nos. 2 through 7) that flow from desire and passion. With

consciousness in particular (No. 4) comes the human quality of awareness of one's contribution to harm to both others and oneself.

The emphasis on unity and harmony might appear to contradict Dostoevsky's burning passion for individuality. But individuality is so crucial to his theodicy that he identifies it as the view of Christ in "The Grand Inquisitor." The harmony or unity of the anthill stands a world apart from the harmony of which Dostoevsky speaks. The Grand Inquisitor charges Christ with having placed freedom "above everything" (253; bk. 5, ch. 5).

> "Instead of taking over men's freedom, you increased it and forever burdened the kingdom of the human soul with its torments. You desired the free love of man, that he should follow you freely, seduced and captivated by you. Instead of the firm ancient law, man had henceforth to decide for himself, with a free heart, what is good and what is evil, having only your image before him as a guide." (255; bk. 5 ch. 5)

The Grand Inquisitor goes on to accuse Christ of leaving human beings with a terrible burden of freedom. By giving freedom of choice to humans, Christ throws them into greater confusion and torment, abandoning them to many cares and insoluble problems (255; bk. 5, ch. 5).

Dostoevsky never wavers in his frankness about the suffering that lies always at the doorstep of freedom. Confusion, torment, suffering, contradiction—without them, freedom cannot conceivably occur. Circumstances deal humans this outrageous collective fortune to bear. It is either the anthill or freedom. Yet if the suffering that comes with freedom is to have meaning, it must in the final analysis offer redemption. Zosima seems to believe that the redemptive suffering of the sins of others as well as one's own sins transports humanity to realms beyond the earthly existence.

> "Much on earth is concealed from us, but in place of it we have been granted a secret, mysterious sense of our living bond with the other world, with the higher heavenly world, and the roots of our thoughts and feelings are not here but in other worlds.... God took seeds from other worlds and sowed them on this earth, and raised up his garden; and everything that could sprout

sprouted, but it lives and grows only through its sense of being
in touch with other mysterious worlds...." (320; bk. 6, ch. 3)

Has Zosima satisfactorily answered the questions raised by Ivan's critique
of Christian theodicy? Early in the story, the narrator assures the reader that
Alyosha, Zosima's disciple, is not a mystic but a realist (25; bk. 1, ch. 5). He
goes so far as to describe him as "clear-eyed and bursting with health," as "even
more of a realist than the rest of us" (25; bk. 1, ch. 5). Zosima's doctrine of
ecstasy, however, seems to fly in the face of this claim; for, after all, Alyosha
knowingly follows in the steps of the Elder, "who takes your soul, your will into
his soul and into his will" (27; bk. 1, ch. 5). Has Dostoevsky allowed himself no
more formidable argument than this: we can find the answer to Ivan only by
having a religious experience? Do Dostoevsky and Zosima fail to see that a
mystical experience might be a grand delusion? The answer, if an answer exists,
lies in Alyosha's leaving the monastery for the very purpose of *testing* the inner
experience of love. The world for Alyosha will act as a laboratory to test what
he believes to be *real*.

Rakitin, a cheap and unworthy mutation of Ivan, scorns Alyosha's despair
over the disappointing fact that the Elder's body decayed prematurely. More
importantly, the premature decay does not uproot the faith of the youthful disciple.
Dostoevsky appears to argue against a faith built upon trivial expectations that have
little to do with the hard and tough gospel of loving one's neighbor. The point of
Dostoevsky's theodicy appears to be that the more one learns to give one's life in
love, the more one learns that a God exists and that he governs the world. In
short, while the mystical experience sets the believer on the right road, it does not
bring him to the end of the road. The believer must test the experience itself in
day-by-day acts of love.

A revealing passage portrays Alyosha as a young man who loves perhaps
in excess. It is an unrestrained love. The whole thrust of the passage nevertheless
reveals this as the starting point of the truly religious life. Dostoevsky's narrator
comes out in the open in defense of his hero:

Nevertheless I shall frankly admit that it would be very difficult
for me now to convey clearly the precise meaning of this strange

and uncertain moment in the life of the hero of my story, whom I love so much and who is still so young. To the rueful question Father Paissy addressed to Alyosha: "Or are you, too, with those of little faith?"—I could, of course answer firmly for Alyosha: "No, he is not with those of little faith." Moreover, it was even quite the opposite: all his dismay arose precisely because his faith was so great.... I would only ask the reader not to be in too great a hurry to laugh at my young man's pure heart. Not only have I no intention of apologizing for him, of excusing and justifying his simple faith on account of his youth, for instance, or the little progress he had made formerly in the study of science, and so on and so forth, but I will do the opposite and declare firmly that I sincerely respect the nature of his heart. No doubt some other young man, who takes his heart's impressions more prudently, who has already learned how to love not ardently but just lukewarmly, whose thoughts, though correct, are too reasonable (and therefore cheap) for his age, such a young man, I say, would avoid what happened to my young man, but in certain cases, really, it is more honorable to yield to some passion, however unwise, if it springs from great love, than not to yield to it at all. Still more so in youth, for a young man who is constantly too reasonable is suspect and of too cheap a price—that is my opinion! (338; bk. 7, ch. 2)

In other words, the realist begins with excessive commitment and in his maturity learns to test and refine his commitment without losing the passion. The pseudo-realist begins with minimal belief and never rises to the world of real life. His criticism has little or nothing to criticize.

Dostoevsky's integrity as a novelist of ideas shines when, immediately after the narrator expresses his view of Alyosha, he allows the narrator to say that Alyosha did not demand a miracle but justice. At this precise point, Alyosha and Ivan meet face to face, for Ivan in the name of justice has already returned his ticket to heaven and the grand harmony. Ivan wishes to have no part in the harmony that traditional theism has advanced over the centuries. This means that the whole thrust of the novel rests on the vision of justice to be embraced.

Alyosha and Ivan start at the same point, demanding justice, and end up in the novel *worlds* apart. Only two pages after demanding "a 'higher justice'" (339; bk. 7, ch. 2), Alyosha says to Rakitin, "I do not rebel against my God, I simply 'do not accept his world'" (341; bk. 7, ch. 2). Alyosha at this point expresses his doubts and of course quotes his brother Ivan. Unquestionably conscious of this artistic move as the author of the novel, Dostoevsky then writes, "Alyosha suddenly smiled crookedly," a descriptive phrase ordinarily reserved for Ivan. Of course, clear-eyed Alyosha recovers both his smile and his faith. Nevertheless, over the present novel hangs still a question mark like a haunting specter. It speaks: Has anyone in this tale truly answered Ivan's contention that the pain and suffering of especially children can never be made right in the grand "harmony?" In Ivan's words, "[T]hey put too high a price on harmony" (245; bk. 5, ch. 5).

Chapter VII. Sacrifice, Tragedy, and Atonement

Christ and the Trojan Horse

Dostoevsky's view of the atonement of Christ will not fit on the traditional Western theological map that places Peter Abelard's theory at one end and Archbishop Anselm's at the other. According to Abelard, Christ's death changed the stony heart of human beings. According to Anselm, Christ's death, serving as sufficient expiation to satisfy the divine honor and holiness, freed God to forgive his sinful creatures. Western Christian theology's doctrines of the atonement did not spring into being by spontaneous generation, but emerged slowly out of ancient Greek and Hebrew traditions, which themselves had roots in the prehistoric struggle of a finite species to come to terms with hostile and friendly forces, both real and imaginary. There can be little doubt that the atonement is a deep-structure theme that has always been widespread if not universal among members of the human species.

Although steeped in ancient Hebrew literature, the New Testament was written in Greek. The Hebrew Bible, translated into Greek almost three centuries before the emergence of Christianity, was used by the early Christians, who, growing up in the Mediterranean world, lived in a time and place permeated by

Greek myths, motifs, tales, stories, and images. The tale of Troy, the basis of the two great Greek epics, found its way into Virgil's *Aeneid,* the popular Roman national epic, perhaps the most influential book composed in Latin. Contained in the *Aeneid* is the popular Trojan horse story that had thrilled adults and children as it passed from generation to generation.

According to the story, Greek soldiers had left their country in order to take Helen out of Troy and return her to her native Sparta. After failing for ten years, the Greeks conceived a trick that promised to bring them victory over the Trojans. They constructed a gigantic wooden horse in whose belly brave Greek warriors lay concealed. The Trojans, seeing the great wooden horse outside the walls of their city, could not resist its allure. They captured the horse and took it inside their fortified city. During the night, the Greek warriors poured out of the belly of the horse and threw open the city gates. The sack of Troy followed.

The oldest theory of Christ's atonement, formulated and taught by the early Church fathers or patristics, presupposed the war model popularized in the Trojan horse story. God and the devil battled one another, not over Helen of Troy, but over the human race itself. Satan had captured the creature that God had made in his own image. As a captive in bondage, humanity could not escape by its finite power. Just as the Greeks in the *Iliad* and the *Odyssey* believed that the gods entered the battle on their behalf, so the early Christian patristics believed that God through Christ had intervened on behalf of his captured human creatures. Before the victory against Satan could be attained, however, Christ of God had to enter into the citadel of evil itself. Since all was fair in war, Christian patristics allowed themselves to believe that God had formed a strategic plan to trick the devil and his underlings in order to defeat them. He sent his own Son to earth to overcome the Prince of Darkness through a clever ploy.

This war model behind the patristics' doctrine of Christ's atonement took on cosmic dimensions in the culture of the first Christian century, which contained the presupposition that the world was populated with demons.

Demonic control of nature was not an esoteric biblical doctrine in first-century Palestine. It was very much the common presupposition of all men of that period, even of most men educated under Greco-Roman auspices. When Celsus, the urbane classicist, attacked Origen he never thought of challenging his view that nature had come under the control of hostile powers. (Wolf 177)

According to the patristics, Satan could not have been expected to volunteer to surrender his prize captive, the human race, without his first receiving an adequate ransom. Augustine did not hesitate to embrace the conclusion drawn earlier by both the Eastern and Western churches that the devil had to be tricked into giving up his hostages. The patristics seemed unclear as to whether God had justified in his own mind the payment of a ransom to Satan. It might well be that their own doubts about such a transaction made it possible for them to justify God's using deception in negotiating with the Father of Lies. Since Satan presumably expected to receive a ransom, God the Heavenly Father sent his Son to appear to be the ransom. What Satan did not know, according to the patristics, was that *the ransom was really bait* by which to trap Satan. In short, God wielded Satan's own weapon of deceit to overcome him and his underlings. Using the analogy of a mousetrap, Augustine portrayed the devil as a mouse, with Christ as the bait on the trap or hook (Driver 41).

The myth as expressed in the Trojan horse motif belonged to the popular culture of the patristics, who portrayed God the Father as not only sending his powerful Son into enemy territory, but also concealing his divinity by casting it in the form of a mortal. Not suspecting that the full power and glory of Heaven had become incarnate in the form of a man, Satan could not resist the bait. Seeing Christ in his apparent state of vulnerability, Satan moved his servants, the rulers of the age, to capture Christ.

Not grasping what was really taking place, the rulers proceeded to capture and execute the Lord of glory. The patristics believed that they had accurately interpreted Paul's meaning in I Corinthians 2:8, which stated that none of the rulers of this age understood God's mystery or secret ploy, "for if they had, they would not have crucified the Lord of glory" (RSV).

Just as the trapdoor to the belly of the Trojan horse opened and the soldiers poured out to defeat the Trojans inside their own fortified city, so Christ's blood, flowing from the cross, became the triumphant power of God inside the enemy's citadel. "He has delivered us from the domain of darkness and transferred us to the kingdom of his beloved Son, in whom we have redemption, the forgiveness of sins" (Col. 1:13 RSV).

The idea that God would offer his Son as a sacrifice to Satan as a payment to effect the ransom or release of the human captives must have struck Augustine as a reversion to the old Manichee dualism that bestowed upon Darkness and Evil a power that threatened to rival the God of Light. By portraying Christ as bait in a trap, however, Augustine could argue that in a contest of power, Satan was no match for the real Sovereign of the universe. Still, by resorting to deceit in dealing with Satan, the God of the patristics appeared to have been forced into a crude version of situation ethics. Augustine would have rejected the explanation that the deception was necessary because the situation was not wholly in God's control. The patristic theory of the atonement nevertheless thrived for centuries.

Christ and Classical Tragedy

In addition to the Trojan horse motif, classical tragedy's theme of suffering and sacrifice influenced the Christian view of the atonement. The assumption of an objective moral order was essential to the ancient Greek tragedy. The performance of the tragedy functioned to remind the audience that doing the right thing and defending the moral order took priority over all other commitments. The critical contradiction or conflict in the tragedy's hero (misleadingly called "character flaw"[1]) led him or her to violate the moral order. Catharsis for the audience came into play when the flawed hero suffered the consequence of either voluntarily or involuntarily violating the moral order or natural order and displeasing the gods.

In *Elements of Tragedy,* Dorothea Krook contends that the act of shame or horror precipitates the central spectacle of suffering in the tragic drama.

> The primary "act of shame" is then seen to be shameful and horrible because it is a violation of a moral order which is objectively real and absolutely binding. The "suffering" precipitated by the act of shame is seen to be not merely

---

[1] We are grateful to Anthony Damico, Professor of Foreign Languages at the University of North Texas, for making this point clear to us.

arbitrary but absolutely necessary, and thus necessary because
expiatory. (17)

According to Krook, the act of violation has to be expiated if the moral
order is to be restored; and the more shameful the violation, "the more intense and
awful the expiatory suffering" (17). The suffering reaffirms the supremacy of the
universal moral order. When the authors of classical tragedy faced the problem
of the moral order, they did not so much doubt its existence or force as affirm it
while they simultaneously explored the relationship between it and the precarious
life of fallible heroes and other mortals who suffered agony and humiliation under
the crushing wheel.

In *The Brothers Karamazov* in particular, Dostoevsky becomes
preoccupied with the whole question of the eternal moral order. He even allows
his philosophical nemesis Ivan Karamazov to suggest the thesis that without belief
in the moral order either the human race would have perished long ago or every
community would have been a hopeless and vicious Gomorrah (238; bk. 5, ch. 4).

No one can read *The Brothers Karamazov* without encountering the thesis
that belief in the moral order is essential to human existence. In the strange and
alluring discussion between Ivan and Alyosha in the tavern, Ivan struggles
personally with this thesis. Like Hamlet, who struggled with the classical
assumption of the objective moral order, Ivan suffers a haunting and subtle
ambivalence regarding the loss of belief in it. Ivan suggests that a child-like part
of him truly does believe in that order. It is the empirical world that God created,
he says, "that I do not accept and cannot agree to accept" (235; bk. 5, ch. 3).

Although convoluted at this point, Ivan's reasoning can be interpreted to
mean that while a part of him wants to accept the eternal moral order, he must
reject the empirical world as unworthy of it. As a dramatic writer and student of
Shakespeare's plays, Dostoevsky understood well the elements of tragedy. In the
attempt to understand his truly original doctrine of atonement, it is imperative to
grasp the fact that in *The Brothers Karamazov* Dostoevsky probes at the heart of
the very concept of tragedy itself. If his final novel is perhaps the greatest
Christian novel in any language, it is because the author does not trivialize human
suffering and agony as if it were mere hiccups of the soul or spiritual growing
pains. By pulling the readers' eyes out of the clouds and back to earth, Ivan
forces the readers to hear the cries and groans of mortals amid glib believers.
While holding the Christian readers' feet to the fire, Ivan proclaims that in every

attempt to transfer human agony into pious heavenly currency, the human race is cheated out of its earnings. In short, he accuses Christian theology of being a cheap, cruel fraud.

When Alyosha mentions the death of "the only sinless One," as somehow a compensation for all the agony and horror suffered on earth, Ivan dismisses the suggestion with moral disgust (240; bk. 5, ch. 4). It must be said that the entire novel stands in firm opposition to what has been called the substitutionary theory of Christ's atonement. It is as if the idea of substitutionary atonement is dismissed as either vulgar phantasmagoria or an analogy empty of moral sensitivity. We suggest that Dostoevsky's view of the atonement came about in part because he not only understood what was at the heart of classical tragedy, but incorporated it into Christianity in a way quite foreign to the somewhat legalistic mind of Anselm, the highly influential Archbishop of Canterbury of the Middle Ages.

Satisfaction and Anselm's Objective Theory of Atonement

The thought pattern of classical tragedy helped to shape and form what theologians label as the *objective theory* of Christ's atonement. The force of Dostoevsky's view of atonement cannot be fully appreciated unless it is seen against the background of the so-called objective theory of Gregory the Great (540-604 C.E.) and Anselm, Archbishop of Canterbury from 1093 to 1109.

According to Gregory the Great, human guilt made an atoning sacrifice necessary. This way of thinking reflects one element of classical tragedy, according to which nothing less than the cosmic moral order had been violated. For Gregory the Great, human sin offended divine holiness. Drawing on the popular penitential system by which saints and martyrs could accumulate more merit than required by Heaven to cover their personal sins, Gregory the Great opened the door to the theory that Christ stored up the most excess merit since he was sinless and therefore needed to offer no penitence for himself.

Archbishop Anselm, however, took this additional step more conspicuously and deliberately. For him, only one person could make the sacrifice sufficient to compensate for all human sin. Striving to be logical and clear about his premises, Anselm began by attacking the various notions of payment or ransom to Satan. Turning patristic theology of the atonement on its head, he argued that Satan was in no position to demand a sacrifice. Satan's honor and holiness had not been offended, since holiness was precisely what he lacked.

Anselm was strongly influenced by the classical tragedy theory that a sacrifice was necessary to restore in some sense the moral order. Adding to this the presupposition of the feudalism of his time, Anselm emerged with the theory that God as the author of all moral order and as the perfection of holiness had been offended by human sin. That is, since God's honor and majesty had been offended, expiation had to be made in order to satisfy the divine honor. Anselm's *satisfaction theory* of the atonement, known also as the *objective theory*, stands in contrast to the *moral influence* theory advanced by Anselm's contemporary, Peter Abelard (1079-1142 C.E.).

Much of Anselm's view of offended majesty became a part of early Protestant theology. In Shakespeare's *Hamlet,* Claudius King of Denmark asks Hamlet if the little play called *The Mousetrap* that has just been performed in their presence contains anything insulting to his majesty (3.2.216). Later, in Scene iii, Rosencrantz reminds King Claudius that the king is not a mere individual but

> That spirit upon whose weal depends
> The lives of many.... Never alone
> Did the King sigh, but with a general groan.

At about the time of the first performance of Shakespeare's *Hamlet,* Hugo Grotius (1583-1645 C.E.) in the Protestant Netherlands conceived a mutation of Anselm's satisfaction theory. Grotius reasoned that Christ's death was not a payment to God for the forgiveness that he freely bestowed, but a tribute to the divine government or the moral order.

Anselm himself, however, had set forth the premise that human sin had to count as *infinite* in its impact because it was an offense *against the honor of the infinite Being.* Indeed, it was also Anselm who argued that the Perfect Being (who could have no conceivable superior) required an expiating sacrifice of nothing less than infinite merit. Furthermore, since *human* sin had so profoundly offended God's honor, a *human* sacrifice was required. Theologians who have defended Anselm's putative objective theory of the atonement have suffered what Freudians will recognize at once as a form of partial denial. It is as if they could not consciously acknowledge the chilling fact that Anselm held that God requires nothing less than *human sacrifice.*

The ancient story of Abraham's willingness to offer his son Isaac as a blood sacrifice to God confronted the practice of human sacrifice and rejected it. Later, the Hebrew woman Hannah presented her son Samuel to God, not as a burnt offering, but to serve as a living priest. Anselm, by contrast, stressed Christ's death as an effective expiation just because it was the death of the perfect specimen of human creation.

Having made it clear in *Cur Deus homo?* that the transgression of God's moral order was an insult to divine honor and dignity, Anselm set out to show why the God-Man came to earth and why he had to die. Anselm failed, however, to show why the perfect man who died had to be possessed also of divinity in addition to humanity. Could not the Omnipotent God have generated a non-divine Second Adam who was perfect as a human being? Anselm's argument raised again the theological issue of the Patripassians, whose view in earlier centuries had forced the Trinitarians to face the question of whether God the Father experienced the sufferings of the God-Man. The Patripassians, while condemned in the West, had considerable influence on the Eastern Church that Dostoevsky regarded as the supreme embodiment of divine revelation. (The question of divine suffering will surface again in the treatment of Dostoevsky's views on Christ's incarnation and the problem of evil.)

Human Sacrifice

Ancient human history abounds with accounts of sacrifices and gifts made to gods and spirits and of favors received from them. One of the more moving stories in Hebrew literature is that of Jephthah, the Hebrew warrior who vowed that if Yahweh would give him a victory over his enemies the Ammonites, he would give to Yahweh as a burnt offering the first creature coming out of his house to meet him upon his return home from victory. His only child—his daughter—was the first to run out to meet him, playing on her tambourine and dancing for joy. Stricken with remorse, Jephthah carried out his vow as if powerless to change his fate.

In the great Greek drama *Oresteia*—a profound theodicy born of a "cruel talent" equal to Dostoevsky's—Aeschylus tells of a sacrifice similar to Jephthah's.

The goddess Artemis, who had rendered the Greek fleet of war idle by subduing the wind, demanded appeasement in the form of the sacrifice of Agamemnon's daughter Iphigenia. Upon receiving the sacrifice, the goddess released the wind and gave the Greek warriors their freedom to resume the battle.

Perhaps no ancient writer excels the Greek playwright Euripides in his *Iphigenia in Tauris* (c. 414 B.C.E.) in the way he probes the motives behind human sacrifice. On one occasion, the goddess Artemis rescues Iphigenia from the raised knife by deceiving the onlookers and substituting a deer in Iphigenia's place.

Sacrifices to the Spirits and Gods

Sacrifices and various forms of appeasement, propitiation, expiation, and atonement to mortals and the immortals go back at least as far as the hunters and gatherers. When the hunters made the kill, they divided the animal's flesh among themselves and their kin and friends. Some believed that ancestors and spirits shared the meal. If it became a sacred meal, it served as something of a proto-Eucharist. To the degree that the early human communities of Cro-Magnon believed that they needed regular sacrifices either to curry the favor of the gods and spirits or to appease their threat to inflict the group with sickness, foul weather or disasters, then to that degree the sacrifices were carried out according to a regular schedule and in proper form.

In a rather primitive and grisly story told in Exodus 4, Yahweh threatens to kill Moses. Zipporah, apparently divining the cause of the threat to her husband's life, picks up a flint and cuts off the foreskin of their son's penis and throws it against Moses' feet. This seems to satisfy Yahweh, who, according to the Exodus account, leaves Moses alone after Zipporah does what is required. The use of flint suggests primitive circumstances and perhaps primitive times, and it is quite possible that circumcision as practiced in its earlier and less schematized form served as an offering to satisfy a god, ancestral spirit, or totem. In the Hebrew Bible, the disparaging references to the Philistines as "uncircumcised" suggests that being circumcised served not only as a sacrifice but as a mark of tribal-totem identity for the Hebrews or a tribe before the Hebrews.

Atonement in the form of full or partial sacrifice has a history in bargaining, negotiating, and appeasing. The early pages of the *Iliad* are profuse with sacrifices and petitions to the gods. Sacrificial grains as well as flesh and red wine are offered as if prepared for a king. On one occasion, when an old man named Chryses prays and sacrifices, Phoebus Apollo hears him.

> When they had made their petitions and scattered the grain, they first drew back the animals' heads, slit their throats, wrapped them in folds of fat and laid raw meat above them. These pieces the old man burnt on the faggots, while he sprinkled red wine over the flames and the young men gathered round him with five-pronged forks in their hands. When the thighs were burnt up and they had tasted the inner parts, they carved the rest into small pieces, pierced them with skewers, roasted them thoroughly, and drew them off. (Homer, *Iliad* 35)

The *Iliad's* narrator reveals that Zeus leaves snow-capped Olympus to keep an appointment in Ethiopia, where a banquet is held in honor of him and all the gods with him. Agamemnon in the *Iliad* makes his people purify themselves by bathing (perhaps a precursor of baptism), and then they offer a rich sacrifice of bulls and goats to Apollo. The savory odors, mixed with curling smoke, go up into the sky.

The Shaman's Boldness

According to the *Odyssey,* the sea-god Poseidon took a trip to the distant Ethiopians to accept a sacrifice of bulls and rams and to enjoy the pleasure of the feast. In other parts of the world, people believed that their ancestors and departed spirits returned to receive gifts as well as to share in the feast. Angry ancestors and spirits received gifts and supplications to ward off their threatened harm. Shamans around the world, however, have typically exercised more boldness than priests in confronting the spirits and gods. They have either believed or led others to believe that they not only could deal with spirits and the departed (who sometimes returned to the tribe), but could transport themselves into the territory of the spirits and the departed souls for the purpose of confronting them face to face. Moses was said to have spoken with God "face to face" (Ex. 33:1). Among both the eastern-most Siberians and the Eskimos, people have gone to their shamans to seek their help in dealing with the spirits face to face.

Shamans have used ventriloquy, impersonations, imitations, drums, and a variety of tricks and deceptions to bring about impressive effects, but that does not mean that they disbelieved in the spirit realm or in their own ability to deal with the spirits. Shamans have sometimes admitted to anthropologists and other outsiders that they have used deceit and trickery in dealing not only with the people, but with especially malevolent spirits and demons. The early patristic notion that God's use of Christ as bait in order to trick the devil probably has its ancestry in the shamans who believed that they had to employ tricks and deception to battle malevolent spirits.

The story of Jacob, a notorious deceiver and trickster, contains the incident of his wrestling all night with someone of mysterious origin and identity. This incident has a ring of a typical nocturnal bout between a shaman and one of the spirits from whom he tries to extract a concession or favor. According to Genesis 32:26, Jacob refused to turn loose of his visitor until he received the visitor's blessing. Jacob received the blessing but not before suffering from the skirmish by having his thigh put out of joint. Jacob concluded that he had seen God face to face.

As the task of attending to the scheduled ceremonial and ritual needs of the gods and spirits became more or less routinized and delegated, the priestly role emerged. Even though the function of putative exorcism is one of the dwindling number of shamanistic functions surviving in the contemporary priestly role, few Catholic or Orthodox priests seem eager to become exorcists. When Roman Catholic priests were stripped of Latin in the Mass, they lost one of the last vestiges of shamanism, since Latin to many of the laypeople seemed to be a special language by which the priests, with their backs to the people, communicated with the realm of the supernatural. As the use of Latin in the Mass was phased out, some priests joined the Charismatic movement, which encouraged both ecstasy and the gift of tongues (speaking in a divine language). Both are traditionally associated with the shamanistic role.

Is the Elder Zosima a Shaman
or a Priest?

In *The Brothers Karamazov,* both the Elder Zosima and Alyosha have their experience of ecstasy. Zosima's famous speech in Book VI, Chapter 1 is strongly stylized and colored with biblical language, Slavonicisms, and the rhetorical diction of eighteenth-century Russian (Terras, *Companion* 246). This distinctive language is not, however, the divine language of the shaman. In fact, Dostoevsky's final and most accomplished novel focuses on the earth and earthly existence far more than the reader is led to expect from Ivan's early insistence that the people need to believe in immortality in order to find meaning and love of neighbor. Indeed, the Elder Zosima comes very close to saying that to practice loving and forgiving one another on earth is the highest ecstasy. Alyosha's transforming ecstasy comes in neither miracles nor the mystical journey through the realm of spirits, but in a surge of joy upon "seeing" God and love in the observable world of trees, birds, flowers, and stars. This is in part what the narrator means when he calls Alyosha a "realist."

In *The Brothers Karamazov,* the priestly role fares no better than does the shamanistic role. Or, more precisely, the priestly role seems to lose its specialized sacerdotal status. The priests no longer function as the exclusive broker of the means of salvation. It is as if the natural and the supernatural have touched so that priests are not needed to link them together. Zosima keeps saying that the actual need is to realize that they already live in paradise. The entire world is sacramental. In *The Possessed,* Bishop Tikhon as more the counselor than the distributor of exclusive soul-saving wafers and wine seems to prefigure Zosima. In short, Dostoevsky, drawing on his Eastern Church tradition, develops a sweeping and full-blown doctrine of Incarnation that starts with God incarnate in nature, albeit not reduced to nature. On this view, there is no need for a priestly class to distribute the grace that is already available for everyone.

God Incarnate

Dostoevsky's theology of the God-filled universe, especially as expounded in *The Brothers Karamazov,* presupposes that the Trinity cannot be so neatly divided that Christ the Second Person of the Godhead came to earth as a man, whereas the other two members of the Trinity somehow avoided the incarnation. Throughout much of his adult life, Dostoevsky wrestled with the need to choose between what he perceived as the two opposing views of the universe:

- The God-less, cannibalistic or reptilian universe and

- The God-filled universe.

Dostoevsky lays out the cannibalistic view in *The Idiot,* where Ippolit, contemplating Holbein's portrayal of Christ dead in the tomb, says:

> Looking at such a picture, one conceives of nature in the shape of an immense, merciless, dumb beast, or more accurately...in the form of a huge machine...which, dull and insensible, has aimlessly clutched, crumbled and swallowed up a great priceless Being, a Being worth all nature and all its laws, worth the whole earth.... This picture expresses and unconsciously suggests to one the conception of such dark, insolent, unreasoning and eternal Power to which everything is in subjection. (389; pt. 3, ch. 6)

The opposite view, expressed most explicitly by the Elder Zosima, portrays the entire physical cosmos as the abode of divinity. In other words, God is incarnate in *all* his creation. Christ then is this incarnation carried out in full love.

The image of Christ in *The Brothers Karamazov* departs radically from Anselm's or Luther's image of someone serving as a crucified sacrifice to appease God's honor and majesty. Dostoevsky's Christ has little in common with Anselm's even though each man regarded himself as a sustained defender of the Christian faith. For Dostoevsky, the sacrificial suffering of Christ cannot be split off from Christ's entire life on earth. In short, there is in Dostoevsky none of the magic of blood found in some versions of the so-called objective theory of the atonement.

In *The Brothers Karamazov,* the Elder Zosima seems at times more like a caring, listening, twentieth-century Rogerian counselor than a priest who mediates the sacraments or reenacts the crucifixion of Christ through the Mass. Indeed, one could easily conclude that throughout *the novel* the idea of suffering and sacrifice comes under heavy scrutiny because *the world has already seen too much suffering and sacrifice*! Certainly Ivan holds to this unmitigated position, made with such unnerving conviction that when Alyosha reminds Ivan that he has forgotten the One who "gave his innocent blood for all and for everything," Ivan replies:

> "Ah, yes, the 'only sinless One' and his blood! No, I have not forgotten about him; on the contrary, I've been wondering all the while why you hadn't brought him up for so long, because in discussions your people usually trot him out first thing." (246; bk. 5, ch. 4)

Instead of Alyosha's picking up the cue, however, a disturbing impression lingers after Ivan has delivered his chilling list of atrocities. The disturbing impression is that Christ's blood does not so much solve the problem of evil as add still another horrible atrocity that counts against the claim that God has created a perfect world. Clearly, Dostoevsky's Christ and the Christianity of *The Brothers Karamazov* will not fit with either Anselm's satisfaction theory of the atonement or the appeasement motif of the ancient Greeks. Dostoevsky's view of atonement goes far beyond both; and if it cannot be reduced to Peter Abelard's moral influence theory of the atonement, then where indeed does Dostoevsky's view fit on the theological map?

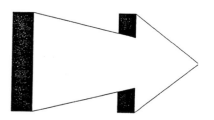

Chapter VIII. Beyond Anselm and Abelard

Peter Abelard's Criticism of the Satisfaction Theory

Even though the view of the atonement in *The Brothers Karamazov* selects elements from most of the major theories set forth by Christian theologians, it bears an originality that prevents it from being reduced to either a mere collection of previous elements or a synthesis. It is no exaggeration to say that Dostoevsky's contribution to the doctrine of atonement is a genuine creative advance.   Its originality can be fully appreciated, however, only against the background of Anselm, Abelard, and their theological heirs.

Peter Abelard (1079-1142 C.E.) subjected Anselm's satisfaction theory to severe criticism. Those in Abelard's camp directed their criticisms primarily at Anselm's notion that the crucifixion of Christ brought about a major change in God that somehow allowed him to forgive repentant sinners. It was not God who needed to be induced to forgive, Abelard reasoned. Rather, human beings needed to be induced to repent and turn in faith to God. Abelard implied that Anselm had seriously misunderstood the nature of God, the whole purpose of the incarnation of Christ, and the meaning of Christ's death on the cross.

Those theologians who have followed what has come to be labeled as Abelard's *moral influence theory of atonement* have taken issue with such heirs of Anselm as Martin Luther and John Calvin, who often spoke of Christ's atonement in legal and forensic terms. According to the *legal or penal theory,* God brought suit against the human race and found it both guilty and deserving of being sentenced to endless torment in hell. Instead of inflicting the punishment on all human beings, however, God directed the fullness of his punishing wrath onto Jesus the Messiah. This transaction, satisfying God's inner standard of justice, is often referred to as the *substitutionary theory* of Christ's atonement.

Two steps occur in this substitution transaction. Not only did infinite human guilt somehow transfer to the innocent Messiah, but the Messiah's infinite righteousness transferred somehow to all sinners who accepted it. Critics raise the question as to whether righteousness can really be transferred like money or possessions from one person to another. Does not righteousness have something to do with the individual's basic character? How can someone whose character is evil be "given" righteousness?

Anselm had set the stage for the arbitrary conclusion that God could not tolerate in the human race anything less than moral perfection. God's honor (Anselm) and justice (Luther and Calvin) required nothing less than moral perfection. Luther and Calvin knew enough about themselves and other believers to know that no Christian could live without moral flaw. Most of the early Protestants were not holiness Christians—they did not believe that the offspring of Adam could in fact reach a state of perfection on earth. Luther and Calvin, despite their awareness of the flaws in the character of believers, followed what they took to be the lead of Paul in the Epistle to the Romans and the Epistle to the Galatians. Briefly stated, the early Protestant Reformers said that Christ's perfection forensically transferred to imperfect believers, which means that even though the believers remained in fact sinful men and women, God treated them *as if* they were morally perfect.

How can this be? Is this a kind of game of hide-and-seek that the Reformers' God plays? Is it pretense? God knows that his human creatures are imperfect and sinful, and yet he *pretends* that they are perfect?   Or is this a manifestation of magical thinking?

Abelard's Moral Influence Theory

Abelard and his theological heirs earlier rejected the legal model in favor of the family relationship model.   According to the latter, the point of the incarnation, of Christ's coming to earth as a human being, was to influence human beings to accept divine forgiveness and fellowship.   The death of Christ on the cross, therefore, served to move the hearts of human beings.   Nothing outside God moved him to forgive, since a forgiving God had sent Christ to live among human beings in the first place.

Criticism of the Moral Influence Theory

The most prevalent charge leveled against Abelard and his theological heirs is that they failed to take human sin seriously.   They failed to recognize that human evil cannot simply be overlooked by a holy and righteous God.   Furthermore, some of Abelard's critics add that the failure to take human sin seriously trivializes all human actions and character.   If human sin does not have an impact on God, then *no human act touches God.   Anselm and his heirs have contended that the impact of human sin is so great as to be infinite in scope.   Consequently, human beings deserve endless torment since they cannot compensate for their infinite sin.   According to Anselm, nothing less than the death of the infinite, incarnated Second Person of the Trinity is* **necessary** in order to rescue at least a portion of the human race from everlasting damnation.

In response to their critics, the followers of Abelard have always contended that, far from ignoring the seriousness of moral evil, their moral influence theory takes sin seriously by trying to do something about it.   The Reformers' abstract forensic righteousness, bestowed by fiat, might serve as a ticket to heaven; but unless the human heart moves toward genuine righteousness, what is heaven but another abode for sinners to carry out their deceit and aggression?   When the Elder Zosima defines hell as the *loss* of the ability to love, he implies that heaven must include the *ability* to love.   The life of Christ, therefore, serves as a model of love; and the death of Christ, for Zosima and the

Abelardians, serves to move people toward the goal of love. When Dostoevsky speaks of the power of "the image of Christ" to move human hearts, he at this one point agrees with Abelard.

Scotus and God's Arbitrary Choice

According to thirteenth-century philosopher Duns Scotus and his theological heirs, nothing necessitated Christ's crucifixion. In the first place, Christ did not have to die on the cross. He might have drowned in the Sea of Galilee. In the second place, God is not a theo-alchemist who must see blood spilled before he can forgive sin. In the third place, the coming of Christ did not bring about a shift in God's being that freed him to release his forgiveness. Duns Scotus reasoned further that since Jesus' suffering was only one person's temporary suffering on a finite scale, God by the arbitrary freedom of his goodness elected to accept Christ's finite suffering as a sufficient sacrifice for sin.

Perhaps more than he had intended, Dun Scotus has thrown open the question of the *arbitrariness* of the entire atonement doctrine. The Lutherans and Calvinists have already admitted that God chose to take the suffering of Christ as atonement and to count Christ's righteousness *as if* it were the righteousness of believers. Is that not arbitrariness?

For those influenced by Scotus, the whole scheme of atonement is built on arbitrariness. What does spilled blood have to do with moral status? Is not the connection so ad hoc as to be a piece of magical rationalization? Far from being objective, Anselm's way of linking the blood or death of one man with the forgiveness of all others turns out to be *egregiously subjective.*

Anselm's subjectivity is perhaps most glaring in his arbitrary, two-fold decision to count human *sin as infinite* and to count human *goodness as at best finite and inconsequential.* To upend Anselm's argument, if he *cannot take human goodness seriously,* he can hardly have reason to inflate human evil to infinite and cosmic proportions. Even when it is granted that Anselm's offended-honor theory is historically conditioned by the feudal concept of royal majesty, the archbishop's notion of human sin as *infinite* does not follow of necessity. Anselm's own vested interest enters into his theology most insidiously at this very point. His theory of atonement is a rigged system set up to make human beings desperately dependent on a priestly class, for in Anselm's time the priests were seen as the necessary brokers of divine grace and forgiveness.

The only necessity in Anselm's theory of atonement, however, is the concocted necessity of having to approach the deity through priestly brokers. Luther's Reformation challenged the indulgence scandal as well as the brokerage. Luther failed, however, to remove the theological scaffolding of the brokerage. For especially the Abelardians, Anselm's theological scheme was from the start a theological monstrosity composed of a collection of ancient myths and motifs that mingled magic with religion. Even worse, it continues to shock elementary human decency.

Dostoevsky on Sacrifice and Suffering

Christians who belong to the Reformed tradition in particular may be tempted to use the atonement theory of Anselm, Luther, and Calvin to interpret Dostoevsky's passages on sacrifice and suffering. They will err if they conclude that Dostoevsky represents those who think that salvation can be earned through the good works and sacrifices made by human mortals. Our purpose is to show how Dostoevsky's position challenges both Protestants and Roman Catholics to look at the whole theme of atonement and salvation in a light different from that of their own traditions. We hope to show also that Dostoevsky has insights into suffering and sacrifice that those who are not Christians will find valuable and fruitful.

Our examination of Anselm's theory of atonement in particular serves to call attention to the way that Dostoevsky's interpretation of the life and death of Christ differs radically from the model that has dominated much of Western Catholicism and Protestantism. In his erudite study of the principal biblical images most intimately connected to the atonement, John Driver exposes several weaknesses of both the Anselmic tradition and the Abelardian tradition (44-65). If Driver's detailed exegesis of both the Hebrew and Christian scriptures regarding the atonement motif is warranted, then Dostoevsky's view of the atonement is more biblical than either Anselm's or Abelard's. Our present task, however, is not to debate what position best conforms to the plurality of relevant biblical texts. Rather, we wish to explicate Dostoevsky's position, spelling it out in detail, so that readers can compare it with other positions, test it for internal coherence, and learn whether it succeeds in solving problems that the traditions of Anselm and

Abelard fail to solve. In short, we focus on Dostoevsky's insights to draw them together as a systematic whole, thereby giving readers the opportunity to test the whole for its philosophical and theological adequacy as well as for its emotional and moral power.

Dostoevsky's position on the atonement does, of course, allow the question: Why was the suffering and death of Christ *necessary*? Arbitrariness seems to plague both Anselm's theory of the atonement and Abelard's. In the case of the latter, it is legitimate to ask: Why was it necessary (rather than arbitrary) for Christ to *die* in order to influence human beings to repent and live in harmony with the Creator and creation? Could not Christ's eyes have been gouged out, leaving him to roam in darkness like a Hebrew Oedipus? In his study of theories of the atonement, William J. Wolf quotes theologian James Denney's criticism of Abelard's moral influence theory:

> "If I were sitting on the end of a pier, on a summer day, enjoying the sunshine and the air, and someone came along and jumped into the water and got drowned 'to prove his love for me' I should find it quite unintelligible. I might be much in need of love, but an act in no rational relation to any of my necessities could not prove it." (Wolf 119-20)

Dostoevsky's theological framework handles the issue of necessity vs. arbitrariness in a way not open to either the Abelardians or those who like James Denney remain in the tradition of Anselm. To make clear Dostoevsky's view on sacrifice and suffering, we will need to provide a sketch of his metaphysics. As early as the 1940s, Philosopher Karl Popper, criticizing the positivists of Vienna, showed that not even science could progress without roots in metaphysics. In the next chapter, we will argue that the similarities between Dostoevsky's metaphysics and what in the United States came to be known as Boston personalism are so striking that by identifying Dostoevsky as a personalist, we render quite meaningful many passages in *The Brothers Karamazov* that have seemed to many readers in the West to be eccentric if not mere Russian sentimentalism or even chauvinism.

Divine Involvement

The key for unlocking the door to Dostoevsky's understanding of Christ's suffering and sacrifice is the doctrine of divine involvement. For Dostoevsky, the incarnation of God in Christ is a part of the broader incarnation of God in nature and in his human creatures. Zosima says that Christ was in the other creatures of the earth before he came to earth as a man. The Word—the everlasting Logos who is Christ—moves all creation so that "every leaf is striving toward the Word, sings glory to God, weeps to Christ, unbeknownst to itself, doing so through the mystery of its sinless life" (295; bk. 6, ch. 2).

By classifying Dostoevsky as a pantheist, Western Christians might think to dismiss the Russian novelist, but in doing so they would mislabel and misconstrue his theology and deprive themselves of a view of sacrifice and suffering that could profoundly challenge their own view. If Dostoevsky embraces, as he seems to, the doctrine of individual responsibility as attributed to the Christ portrayed in "The Legend of the Grand Inquisitor," then no one can support the claim that Dostoevsky's Christian psychology and theology drifts into pantheism. The robustness of Dostoevsky's theology lies in his willingness to see the deity in the world, not as an absentee landlord who in the first century sent his Son to visit a dilapidated apartment, but as the Creator perpetually incarnate in his own manifest splendor.

For decades, Dostoevsky scholars have puzzled over the question of whether Ivan Karamazov is really an atheist. We advance the thesis that the narrator of *The Brothers Karamazov* judges Ivan to be in a state of rebellion or mutiny because Ivan in effect rejects the broader doctrine of the Creator's incarnation in the world. This rejection of the world is not so much atheism as an extreme doctrine of transcendence or deism that denies any abiding identity or connection between God and the world. Christ's appearance on earth is, for Dostoevsky, not so much the deity descending to earth like an Olympian divinity who commutes and then later sends a second divinity, the Spirit, to replace the first. Rather, Christ's appearance in human form is a further manifestation of divine grace. God could be "in Christ reconciling the world to himself" (2 Cor. 5:19 RSV) only if he were from the beginning in the world manifesting his glory, grace, and splendor. The appearance of the Son is meaningless without the slanting rays of the sun that warm the earth and inspire the human heart.

From Dostoevsky's perspective, divine reconciliation did not begin with the appearance of Christ in human form. Rather, the appearance of Christ is the ceaseless incarnation of God intensified, God's "identification" with his human creation becoming even more manifest. If the sorrows of human beings have always been in some sense God's sorrows, too, then the sufferings and sacrifice of Christ—the supreme human manifestation of God's presence—serve to emphasize that the cross has always been in the heart of the Creator. Dostoevsky thus solves the problem of the *necessity* of Christ's suffering. The necessity is fundamentally a question of becoming personally involved in human existence. To become involved deeply and directly in human experience is to face suffering and death *inevitably*.

If God chose to participate directly in human experience by the intensity of personal incarnation, he chose by implication to face suffering and death. This means that the necessity of Christ's death turns out to be its inescapability. In that respect, Christ's death became the crowning test and proof of the Creator's supreme involvement in human experience. Far from thinking of Christ's death as a magical transaction of expiation effecting forgiveness, however, Dostoevsky views it as the inevitable outcome of assuming mortal flesh. Christ's death is divine *involvement* carried out with full obedience to his own divine commitment to become fully human. If the sacrifice of Christ means anything, it means that it *cost God* to become intimately involved in human experience and community. This is not to suggest that a price was paid to putative demons. Rather, there was risk in becoming compassionately involved in human flesh and conflict, which inescapably led to suffering and sacrifice. Accordingly, God's appearing in human form is the sacrifice made, not as expiation or an appeasement either of Satan or of himself, but because to become human to live as the supreme manifestation of goodness on earth is to endure the slings and arrows of outrageous human modality.

In *The Idiot,* Prince Myshkin—the Prince of peace in the story—is crushed by the human conflict. Indeed, the sense of inevitability found in some of the Greek tragedies pervades the account of the Prince's apparent dissolution. And yet, his last act in the story is an act of Christ-like compassion.

The Problem of Human Sacrifice

The proponents of Anselm's so-called objective theory of the atonement have yet to come to terms with the charge that according to Anselm's doctrine, God the Father required human sacrifice. Dostoevsky's Elder Zosima does not have Anselm's problem for the plain reason that they do not share the same view of sacrifice. For Zosima, sacrifice is an unavoidable dimension of loving involvement. Since conflict is inevitable in human interaction—indeed each individual experiences self-conflict—each person will absorb from all others the consequences of emerging pride, deceit, treachery, jealousy, as well as frustration, misjudgment, misunderstanding, and other manifestations of human finitude. Instead of becoming an appeasement or an expiation, Christ's sacrifice was that of submitting to become involved directly in the human condition in order to bring about reconciliation.

The Anselmic tradition and Dostoevsky's view are a world apart. Dostoevsky rejects the commercial and legal transaction that the Anselmic tradition suggests. He is much closer to the personalism of Borden Parker Bowne, who came to Germany to study the philosophy of Rudolf Lotze in the year that Dostoevsky left Germany for Russia. Years later, having returned to his position at Boston University, Bowne wrote in a chapter titled "Incarnation and Atonement" words that agree perfectly with Zosima's own position:

> Vicarious suffering and vicarious sacrifice abound in life, owing to the solidarity of life and especially to the solidarity of love, but there is a world-wide difference between them and *vicarious* punishment. The former we all accept as love's greatest manifestation; the latter is the caricature by mechanical minds of love's supreme manifestation, so as to turn God's grace itself into one of the great stumbling-blocks to its acceptance. (134)

Bowne and Dostoevsky, who probably never met one another in Germany, came together nevertheless in thought regarding the purpose of the incarnation of Christ. It was not to bring about formal or forensic goodness, but to develop goodness of heart that leads to genuine repentance of evildoing. It was not an abstract and magical exchange in some spiritual hinterland. Neither Bowne nor Dostoevsky is "soft" on moral evil. Their point is that genuine salvation and redemption must include good works, not to earn the divine grace that is freely given, but because goodness, beauty, and moral laws and consequences belong organically to the "largeness and richness and fullness of life itself" (Bowne 150).

Chapter IX. Incarnation and Personalism

Dostoevsky's Vision of the Cosmic Incarnation

Elder Zosima stands a world apart from those patristics in particular who saw Creation as in bondage to the Power of Darkness until the coming of Christ. Augustine set out to answer the question of how it came to be that the Cosmic Criminal took over the Creator's world. During his years in the Manichee faith, he assumed that the God of Light had never enjoyed full control of the world in the first place.

Through Zosima, Dostoevsky unveils his position that God has always been incarnate in the world. This must be understood as more than the general doctrine of divine immanence. Sufficient evidence exists in especially *The Brothers Karamazov* to strengthen the hypothesis that Dostoevsky is not a pantheist, but a *theistic personalist*. The common factor between these two views is that each emphasizes the intimacy between God and nature. American personalism in particular differs sharply from pantheism, however, by treating each center of finite consciousness as a unique self, unabsorbed into the Cosmic Consciousness or Mind of God. Dostoevsky's critics who try to force him into the

pantheistic camp do so perhaps because they lack awareness of the details of the Boston personalism of B. P. Bowne, E. S. Brightman, and Peter A. Bertocci.

To interpret the Elder as a theistic personalist is to shed light on Dostoevsky's fascination with the sticky leaves, the stars, the flowers, and the snow. Even though an urbanite of St. Petersburg, Dostoevsky believed he could "see" the world as God's own presence. Bowne, a contemporary of William James, advanced the thesis that nature is the energizing of God. Human organisms, like the organisms of all other species, are pockets of divine energy that serve as the base from which evolves distinctive streams of consciousness. Like Dostoevsky, the Boston personalists wrestled all their adult lives with the crucial philosophical problem of the one and the many. For the personalists, the physical system of nature is in reality the unified energy of God without which the vast plurality of centers of consciousness would have no means of interacting and communicating with one another.

The birds, for example, like human beings, share in God's energy because they too have bodies. According to personalism, each creature also has its own special degree and quality of subjective experience emerging from its body. The finite body is the function of consciousness, just as consciousness is the function of the body. God's supreme consciousness is distinct from each finite center of consciousness even though no finite life could exist apart from the energizing of God, which is nature.[1]

Theistic personalism, by taking all of nature both seriously and sacramentally, has no need of mystical flights. Similarly, Dostoevsky's young hero and the Elder seem to find most of their ecstasy in perceiving God and joy manifest in nature. Giving no comfort to those mystics who denigrate the senses, personalists regard the senses to be the mind's taproot in and link to nature; and since nature is divine energizing, the senses are the avenues by which God sustains perpetual communication with all finite creatures. No one needs a private interview with the Creator for the simple reason that divine revelation is both

---

[1]The panentheism of Charles Hartshorne and A. N. Whitehead has much in common with the metaphysics of such personalists as E. S. Brightman and Peter A. Bertocci. Brightman and Bertocci as epistemological dualists, however, reject Hartshorne's claim that God, while having his own unique and infinite experience, *possesses* the subjective states of all finite centers of consciousness.

public and everywhere. All nature sings and rings with divine beauty and grace for those who can properly interpret what their senses deliver.

According to the personalistic interpretation, God has always been incarnate in the world. God's perpetual, manifest energy is in the song of a bird, in the cry of the wolf, or in thunder and rain. The earth that Zosima and Alyosha water with their tears is God's own body, for nature is the body of God, with Mother Earth as God's nourishing bosom.

In an exceedingly insightful but somewhat petulant article entitled "The Religious Dimension: Vision or Evasion? Zosima's Discourse in *The Brothers Karamazov*," the noted Dostoevsky scholar Sergei Hackel seems genuinely puzzled over what he calls Zosima's "veneration of the earth" and refers somewhat sarcastically to "a cult of the earth..." (144-7). Hackel's puzzlement could perhaps have vanished if he had been able to see Dostoevsky as a theistic personalist whose love of nature is at least a partial love of God. Zosima's treatment of the earth as sacred stems from his understanding of the intimate connection between God and nature in Eastern Orthodoxy. Hackel himself notes that since the days of the patristics, the Eastern Orthodox Church "has preserved an understanding of Creation which involves no rigid separation between nature and grace" (146). Boston personalism restored divine revelation to nature at a time when Protestant fundamentalism had tried to reduce revelation to the pages of a book. Hackel's apparent puzzlement over the earth's being treated as sacred dissolves once Dostoevsky is understood to be more a personalist than a pantheist.

For the personalists, God's mind does not absorb finite minds in pantheistic fashion, for such absorption is quite unnecessary. God and all human creatures share nature joyfully, and to understand this is to understand that the meaning-of-life question dissolves. Dmitri Karamazov, feeling his own joy, quotes from Schiller's "Ode to Joy":

> Joy is the mainspring of the whole
> Of endless Nature's calm rotation;
> Joy moves the dazzling wheels that roll
> Within the great heart of creation....
> All being drinks the mother-dew
> Of joy from Nature's bosom....
> (107; bk. 3, ch. 3)

Theistic personalism, by seeing nature as "the body and garment of God," makes of nature a perpetual sacrament, a means of divine grace. Significantly, Zosima's last act on earth is not that of receiving the ecclesiastical rite. Rather, "he—suffering but still looking at them with a smile—silently lowered himself..., then bowed down with his face to the ground, stretched out his arms, and as if in joyful ecstacy, kissing the earth and praying (as he himself taught), quietly and joyfully gave up his soul to God" (324; bk. 6, ch. 3).

The Humanity of God

The author of the Epistle to the Hebrews portrays Christ as the high priest who, having suffered temptation on earth, can now be "touched with the feeling of our infirmities" (Heb. 4:15 KJV) or "sympathize with our weaknesses" (RSV). The author goes on to urge his readers to approach the throne of grace with confidence or boldness, since God or at least Christ will understand the finite human condition (4:16). Employing this and other passages in the New Testament, some Christian theologians have argued that through Christ's incarnation not only did God enter more fully the world and human life, but also humanity passed into the life of the Godhead.

Zosima's God is not Calvin's Monarch or Sovereign who has no real contact with the feelings and sufferings of humanity. In Calvin's theology, the sacrifice of Christ is designed more to satisfy God's holy wrath than to provide God with a way to take on the feelings of humanity. Western Christian theology has traditionally been exceedingly dubious of the possibility of God's taking the human experience into himself. By splitting off the Son to come to earth, however, Western Christianity in particular has seemingly allowed only one member of the Trinity to take on humanity, including suffering, feelings of trepidation, uncertainty, the sense of danger, and even despair. The idea of the Heavenly Father's suffering or feeling anything human has troubled a number of influential Western theologians. Ironically, Calvin's God, even though formally the omniscient one, gives to theology a celestial Monarch who knows everything except what it feels like personally to be a finite human being. He is a Monarch out of touch with his subjects. Indeed, in the secret counsel of his thoughts, he elects to redeem some and to damn others. He is the Sovereign, the Potter; and human creatures are his clay to do with them whatever he wills (Rom. 9:11-24).

Calvin and other heirs of Anselm imply strongly that the atonement of Christ on the cross objectively affected God or changed something in God the Father that allowed his grace to flow freely. At the same time, they insist that the *daily life of Christ incarnate* added nothing to God the Father, making not a ripple in his Eternal Parmenidean Oneness.

By contrast, Zosima and Alyosha appear to think not only that they are touched by God, but also that they *literally touch and move God* when they kiss the earth and water it with their tears. To alien eyes, such an act might seem to be sentimental drivel. The type of Puritan who has yet to come to terms with human sensuality might call this act idolatry. The type of secularist who cannot see meanings outside his or her own world view might deem Zosima's and Alyosha's falling to the earth and kissing it to be a self-degrading act of supplication at best or a disgusting act of toadyism at worst. Dostoevsky, however, judges this act to be none of these. It is imperative to understand that Dostoevsky's theology does not project a deity on the model of Calvin's male monarch. For Dostoevsky, the earth as a part of God's own garment or body is Mother Earth. When in a moment of great crisis Alyosha throws himself to the earth, he is as a child throwing himself into his mother's arms.

> He did not know why he was embracing it, he did not try to understand why he longed so irresistibly to kiss it, to kiss all of it, but he was kissing it, weeping, sobbing, and watering it with his tears, and he vowed ecstatically to love it, to love it unto ages of ages. "Water the earth with the tears of your joy, and love those tears...," rang in his soul.... He wanted to forgive everyone and for everything, and to ask forgiveness, oh, not for himself! but for all and for everything, "as others are asking for me," rang again in his soul. (362; bk. 7, ch. 4)

This spontaneous act of watering the earth with tears of joy and of kissing and embracing the earth is not to be taken as either mere eccentric behavior or unnatural theatrics. Rather, nothing is more natural than this to people like Zosima and Alyosha, who believe they are literally touching the Creator at every moment. When the tears soak into the earth, they touch and move God, literally returning some of themselves to Mother Earth.

We suggest further that when Dostoevsky and his narrator in *The Brothers Karamazov* speak of Alyosha as a realist and not a mystic, they mean to imply that Alyosha is truly at home on earth, in the world. It is on earth and among earth's people that Alyosha really meets God and serves him. Zosima does not promise the young realist that his "sojourn in the world" (363; bk. 7, ch. 4) will be free of pain. To the contrary, he warns, "Life will bring you many misfortunes..." (285; bk. 6, ch. 1). It is not masochistic need but realism that prompts Zosima to tell Alyosha that through his misfortunes he will be happy and will bless life and cause others to bless it. This is simply the way life works. Once original conflict and the surging passion of life come into being, suffering becomes a part of "the law of our planet" (*Notebooks for <u>Crime</u>* 188). "'Except a corn of wheat fall into the ground and die, it abideth alone: but if it die, it bringeth forth much fruit'" (285; bk. 6, ch. 1).

Clearly, Dostoevsky in *The Brothers Karamazov* presupposes divine-human interactionism, each enriching the other. God creates and relates perpetually to Creation, not because of external necessity, but because God is love and because it is the nature of divine love to create, to share, and to become involved even when the involvement leads to suffering.

Mother Earth

The *Apocryphon of John* speaks of Father, Mother, and Son. Elaine Pagels notes that the *Gospel to the Hebrews* portrays Jesus as speaking of "my Mother, the Spirit." The *Secret Book,* quoted by Pagels, speaks of "the Mother of everything, for she existed before them all, the mother-father [*matropater*]..." (62). Even though some of the all-male clergy of the Western Catholic tradition set out to repress texts that speak of the feminine depth of divinity, some of the texts survived. The Mother Earth image serves Dostoevsky well by including both that which is created and that which generates and creates. Dostoevsky seems to treat the earth as well as the "innumerable worlds" (362; bk. 7, ch. 4) as God's perpetual manifestation. While God is not reduced to the earth or to any manifestation, it is of the essence of deity to live manifestly and in relationships. When Zosima quotes with approval his brother's statement that they are all in paradise, this must be taken at face value. Paradise is not in some other "place"

or "realm." To the contrary, paradise, or this local aspect of it, is here and now because human beings live on Mother Earth, the extension and symbol of divine manifestation. The act of watering the earth with tears, therefore, is a celebration—"tears of joy"—and an overflow of love, not the act of a sycophant.

Far from being something that Dostoevsky discovered while writing *The Brothers Karamazov,* the idea of Mother Earth lay deep in his Russian heart. A decade before the publication of his last novel, Dostoevsky worked on the shocking novel *The Possessed.* In it he raises the question of the relationship between God and nature and has one of his characters exclaim, "God and nature are one and the same thing" (139; pt. 2, ch. 4). Another character in *The Possessed,* however, gives voice to a position that more accurately expresses the position that Zosima later seems to presuppose:

> "'You're right there,' she said to me. 'The Mother of God is our great mother earth, and there's great happiness for me in that. And in every sorrow and in every earthly tear there's happiness for us. And once you've soaked the earth a foot deep with your tears, you'll rejoice in everything right away....'
>
> "Those words touched me deep down inside and I began then, when I knelt down to pray, to kiss the earth, and every time I kissed it I wept.... I climbed that mountain [Pointed Mountain], faced the east, and kissed the ground; and I cried and cried and didn't even know how long I stayed there crying or what was happening around me. Then I got up and turned around and watched the sun setting, so big and velvety and so pretty." (140; pt. 2, ch. 4)

According to Erik Krag in *Dostoevsky: The Literary Artist,* Dostoevsky shared with many Russians, the ancient Greeks, and the German poet Schiller a belief in Mother Earth as a living reality. The planet is the Great Mother, "the bearer of the life of us all" (129). F. C. Cornford interprets the Greek philosopher Plato in *Timaeus* to mean that the World-soul is embodied in the universe or World-body:

We have been told that the World's body has no sense organs, because there is nothing outside it to be perceived. But the World's Soul is not pure intelligence; being united with a perceptible body, it may be imagined as having internal feelings, which would be covered by the word *aesthesis*. (96)

In Dostoevsky's *Crime and Punishment,* the name of the protagonist Raskolnikov stems for the root *raskol,* which means "separation" or "schism." Raskolnikov is already an alienated being before he commits murder, his alienation consisting of a revolt against Mother Earth and the world order. Like Orestes in Aeschylus' *Oresteia,* Raskolnikov suffers, eventually gains knowledge (insight), and kisses the earth in the process of confessing his evildoing. Toward the end of *Crime and Punishment,* Sonya, the young woman who loves him, implores Raskolnikov to go to the town square to "bow down to people, kiss the earth, because you have sinned before it as well, and say aloud to the whole world: 'I am a murderer!'" (525; pt. 6, ch. 8)[1]

When the phrase "Mother of God" appears in Dostoevsky's novels, the image often fuses with the popular feeling toward Mother Earth that was both still alive among the Russian peasantry and dear to Dostoevsky's heart. *Zemlia* (earth) is feminine in Russian. The Russian name *Dmitri* is from the Greek *Demetrios,*

---

[1]Zosima's portrayal of nature (without the human species) as a harmony containing both conflict and suffering resembles, ironically, Adam Smith's vision of the free market. For Smith, the intrusion of government is the original sin of economics and a prime source of numerous personal and public agonies. In laissez faire capitalism lies the ideal balance or harmony of commerce and economic interchange. The balance is so remarkable that it gives the appearance of being the product of Providence, the invisible hand. Similarly, for Zosima, nature apart from the interference of human pride, greed, spite, and other human vices enjoys perfect balance and harmony despite the conflict and suffering. Zosima exclaims:

"Love the animals: God gave them the rudiments of thought and an untroubled joy. Do not trouble it, do not torment them, do not take joy from them, do not go against God's purpose. Man does not exist above the animals: they are sinless, and you, with your grandeur, fester the earth by your appearance on it, and leave your festering traces behind you—alas, almost everyone of us does!" (319; bk. 6, ch. 3)

derived from **Demeter** (lit. "Mother Earth"). The Eleusinian mysteries were celebrated in honor of Demeter and were close to being a natural religion of the earth (Terras, **Companion** 117).

Unlike Ivan, Dmitri, as befits his name, accepts the earth and the world and quotes from Schiller's poem "The Eleusinian Festival."

> "That men to man again may soar,
>   Let man and Earth with one another
> Make a compact evermore—
>   Man the son, and Earth the mother...."
> (107; bk. 3, ch. 3)

The Eleusinian mysteries, celebrated annually in honor of Demeter and her daughter Persephone, symbolized the annual death and resurrection of nature. What is crucial to understand about Dostoevsky's personalism is that the planet Earth belongs to and is a symbol of all the divine manifestations. It gains life and meaning in connection with "the other worlds" (320; bk. 6, ch. 2). Knowing that much on earth is concealed from them, human beings sense that the earth has "a living bond with the other world" (320; bk. 6, ch. 2). For Alyosha, who represents the best of Dostoevsky's beloved Greek Orthodox Church, there is continuity in all creation, the seamless divine garment. "The silence of the earth seemed to merge with the silence of the heavens, the mystery of the earth touched the mystery of the stars." When Alyosha embraces the earth and waters it with his tears, the vault of heaven descends into his soul" (362-3; bk. 7, ch. 4).

At the end of Book Three of **War and Peace,** Tolstoy's young soldier Andrew Bolkonski undergoes a transformation, too, as he, lying wounded on the battlefield, looks up at the lofty, equitable, and kindly sky. When Napoleon steps up to him, the greatness of Bonaparte seems insignificant when compared with the infinite sky. Tolstoy and Dostoevsky, each in his distinctive way, are saying that nature evokes the **mysterium tremendum** and a fascination that can lead at least some individuals to "see" in a way they had never before seen.

More than Tolstoy, Dostoevsky is perhaps the heir of the ancient Greek notion that all things are in some sense full of the gods. Thales, the first philosopher of the West, may have thought that soul was distributed throughout the universe. The ever-elusive Plato, speaking of the stars as gods to be honored, claims that for Proclus the cosmos was the holiest of shrines or receptors of

divinity. In his Platonist period, even Aristotle regarded the heavenly bodies, including the planets, as gods enjoying voluntary motion. Plato in *Laws* (898D) speaks both of heavenly bodies moved by an individual soul and of the Soul that drives the whole heaven around (Cornford 100-1, 108). Plato often spoke poetically, with his key words becoming metaphors or his theories more mythic mutants than systematic cosmology. But at least Plato's readers understood the universe to be divinity saturated. The celestial bodies, including Earth, are "everlasting and divine." Earth itself is called "our nurse and...[the] most venerable of all the gods that are within the heavens" (*Timaeus* 40B-C).

The God-Bearing Nation

The Greek playwright Aeschylus (525—456 B.C.E.), extolling Athens as a place where the gods were pleased to dwell, calls Athens a jewel flashing forth anew (*Eumenides* 920). In *War and Peace,* His Lordship the Bishop sends a letter of ecclesiastical, patriotic eloquence to the Emperor: "Moscow, our ancient capital, the New Jerusalem, receives *her* Christ as a mother receives her zealous sons into her arms..." (1040; bk. 12, ch. 1). Unlike Dostoevsky, Tolstoy came to abhor the fusion of nationalism and religion. For Dostoevsky, God is not only incarnate in creation, but also in the Russian peasantry and Russian soil in particular. If Europeans thought of themselves as the enlightened ones who could save barbaric Russia from her backwardness, Dostoevsky from around 1863 to 1881 came to believe passionately that the true gospel had been preserved by the peasants of the Greek Orthodox Church and that Russia had been selected by God to serve as the agent by which Europe—the graveyard—could be saved and resurrected to new life and salvation. It is imperative to understand that Dostoevsky believed literally in the incarnation of God on earth, just as many of the ancient Greeks believed that the greater deities of the ancient pantheon dwelled on nearby Mt. Olympus.

The fusion of ethos and religion thrived in the United States in the era of Dostoevsky and Tolstoy. Many Christians in the eighteenth and nineteenth centuries looked upon the United States not only as the land flowing with opportunity, but also as the New Israel, as God's chosen instrument to serve as a model and light to the nations. The popular preacher and writer Alexander Campbell saw Great Britain and the United States as a united terrestrial agent of

God anointed to distribute God's ways, including salvation, to the unenlightened. In 1849, the year of Dostoevsky's arrest, Campbell gave his "Address on the Anglo-Saxon Language," in which he made glowing predictions:

> The Lord Almighty, who has now girdled the earth from east to west with the Anglo-Saxon people, the Anglo-Saxon tongue, sciences, learning and civilization, by giving a colossal power and grandeur to Great Britain and the United States over continents and oceans of the earth, will continue to extend the power and magnificence until they spread from north to south, as they have already from east to west, until, in one vernacular, in one language and with one consent they shall, in loud acclaim and in hallowed concert, raise their joyful and grateful anthem...to the ends of the earth. Then will "they hang their trumpet in the hall, and study war no more." Peace and universal amity will reign triumphant. For over all the earth there will be but one Lord, one faith, one hope, and one language. (*Popular* 44)

Only Dostoevsky's boundless nationalism and pan-Slavism could match Campbell's postmillennial faith.

In the 1850s, Dostoevsky welcomed European influences because he believed that circumstances had selected the Russian mind to be the great synthesizer of science and learning flowing in from the other nations. He never gave up his conviction that the Russian people embodied the unique characteristic of being truly universal. He became increasingly nationalistic just because he believed that Europe had lost her soul. Only Russia remained to become the shepherd of the greatest possible cultural diversity. Like the Russian poet Pushkin, Dostoevsky claimed that the real strength of the Russian national spirit was its drive toward universality and all-embracing humanitarianism (Dowler 174).

In *The Possessed*, which first appeared in a St. Petersburg monthly in 1871-72, the grumpy but honest character named Shatov represents Dostoevsky's position more than does any other character in the story. Shatov refers to Russia as "the one and only God-bearing nation on earth, destined to regenerate and save the world in the name of the new God—the nation that alone holds the keys of life and the New World" (234; pt. 2, ch. 1). In another passage only a few pages

later, the same Shatov gives voice to a heady theory of the relationship between the nations and their gods. Perhaps no passage in all of Dostoevsky's novels expresses so bluntly his controversial native-soil theology:

> "So now I'm reducing God to a national attribute, am I?" Shatov shouted. "It's just the other way around; I'm raising the nation to God. And indeed, has it ever been otherwise? *A people forms the body of its god.* A nation is a nation only so long as it has its particular god and excludes as irreconcilable all other gods; so long as it believes that with the help of its god it will conquer and destroy all other gods. All great nations have so believed since the beginning of time—at least all who have left their mark as nations, who have led mankind. It is impossible to dismiss the fact. The Jews lived only to await the coming of the true God and they left the true God to the world. The Greeks worshipped nature and bequeathed their religion to the world—their philosophy and art. Rome deified the state and left the concept of the state as a legacy to the nations. France, during her long history, has been nothing but the incarnation and elaboration of the concept of the Romanish god and if she has now gone over to atheism—which they call socialism over there—it is because even atheism is healthier than Roman Catholicism. If a great nation does not believe that it alone to the exclusion of any other possesses the sole truth, if it does not believe that it alone is destined to and can regenerate and save the rest of the world through the truth it holds, it immediately ceases to become a great nation and becomes merely an ethnographical designation. But there is only one truth and therefore only one people can possess it and, with it, the only true God, though other peoples may have their own particular gods, even great ones. Now, the only God-bearing nation is the Russian nation...." (238; pt. 2, ch. 1. Italics added)

Shatov, pressed by the decadent Nikolai Stavrogin, confesses that he believes the new coming of Christ will take place in Russia. He seems to identify

Russia and the Russian Orthodox Church as the New Testament version of the "body of Christ" (239; pt. 2, ch. 1).[1]

Perfect consistency in Dostoevsky's theology of nationalism gave way to a tension between two opposing views. On the one hand, he portrayed Russia as the nation in which the contributions of other nations could receive maximum understanding, appreciation, and celebration. The earlier Dostoevsky proclaimed the ideal of reconciliation between East and West. In *The Notebooks for A Raw Youth*, he wrote: "Europe will give us science, and we will give Christ to them; in this is Russia's whole purpose" (Dowler 172). He called Pushkin "the national" in the highest sense of the word because the great poet, Dostoevsky believed, had the Russian ability to understand profoundly the truths of other lands and to give them universality (Dowler 125-6, 174).

On the other hand, Dostoevsky slipped into jingoism and for a while an exclusivistic nationalism. Two 1877 articles of *The Diary of a Writer* ring with militaristic rhetoric that is alien to the spirit of Alyosha and Zosima (626-37). Russia was at war with the Turks in that year; and, as Geir Kjetsaa notes, it was difficult to remain a pacifist in an uncommonly bloody war with the Turks, who were alleged to have impaled infants on bayonets while the helpless parents watched (332).[2]

In *The Brothers Karamazov*, jingoism gives way to the gospel of Christian humanism. Dostoevsky's earlier image of the "God-bearing" people must not be confused with that of a master race. On the whole, as Dostoevsky moved increasingly toward nationalism, his concept of nationalism transformed into the religious ideal identified with a tolerant Orthodox Christianity as practiced more or less faithfully by the common people of Russia. One student of Dostoevsky's native-soil religion offers the following succinct comment:

---

[1]Ephesians 5:23 and Colossians 1:18, 24 refer to the church as Christ's *body*. Dostoevsky, regarding the Russian Orthodox Church as the true Church, did not always draw a sharp line between his Church and Russia. At times, Dostoevsky seemed to have an almost mystical notion of the Russian people as one personality receiving the Divine Logos (Ivanov 57-60).

[2]In *War and Peace*, Tolstoy chides historians who equate the welfare of the French, Germans, and English with "the civilization of all humanity, by which is usually meant the peoples inhabiting a small, northwestern corner of the great mother earth" (Garnett translation). The Maude translation reads: "...a small northwesterly portion of a large continent" (1314; Second Epilogue).

In his middle and later years...Dostoevsky came to believe in a
universal mission for Russia. Through Orthodox Christianity,
he believed, all the conflicts of civilization would be reconciled.
Hence in Dostoevsky reconciliation came to mean the
reconciliation of East and West in universal Christian harmony.
(Dowler 179)

In the United States, comparable hopes among Protestants rose to
rapturous heights. In *The Evidences of Christianity*, which records his 1829
debate with socialist Robert Owen, the Protestant preacher Alexander Campbell
heralded his sanguine anticipation of "a restoration of the ancient order of things,
and a state of society far superior to anything yet exhibited on earth" (395). In
eloquence designed to overpower Owen's vision of the ideal society, Campbell
broke out in a panegyric of the Christian-controlled millennium on earth:

Fancy yourselves, my friends, a society in which such
characteristics shall have rule, and then you want [i.e., need] no
poet to describe the millennium to you. Peace, harmony, love,
and universal good-will must be the order of the day. There
wants nothing—believe me, my friends, there wants nothing—but
a restoration of ancient christianity, and a cordial reception of it,
to fill the world with all the happiness, physical, intellectual, and
moral, which beings like us in this state of trial could
endure—shall I say?—yes, endure, and enjoy. (385)

In 1849, in a sermon titled "The Destiny of Our Country," Campbell,
disturbed by the threat of Roman Catholics and other immigrants pouring onto
American shores, wrote:

We will by common schools and common ministrations of
benevolence, dispose them of the demon of priestcraft and
kingcraft, and show them our religion by pointing to our
common schools, our common churches, our common colleges,
and our common respect for the Bible, the Christian religion and

its divine and glorious Founder—the supreme Philanthropist. (*Popular* 181)

Early sixteenth-century Puritans of New England looked upon themselves as the New Israel. Joseph Smith, a contemporary of Alexander Campbell in the early nineteenth century, saw himself and his fellow Mormons as the new "Zion" in the new world. Whereas Campbell spoke of restoring New Testament Christianity to the land, Smith spoke of restoring the temple of Israel and the priesthood of Aaron through the work of the new chosen people, the Latter Day Saints (Shipps 81-3).

Dostoevsky, no less than many of the Puritans, Campbellites, and Mormons in the United States, looked upon the Jews as the fallen people. Like other Christians of the West, Dostoevsky looked forward to the day that the Jews would ultimately be saved by a universal communion in the name of Christ. The mantle of the Old Israel, fallen Israel, had been bestowed, Dostoevsky believed, upon the New Israel, Holy Russia. When he spoke of the "Russian Christ" and the "Russian God," Dostoevsky voiced his conviction that God not only was incarnate in his creation, but had also chosen the people of Holy Russia to be his theophanic people (Goldstein 162-3).

The Image of Christ

Dostoevsky's metaphysics of personalism highlights the far-reaching extent of divine incarnation in his theology. What can be said, however, of the specific incarnation of Christ?

The appearance of Christ in human life and form was not for Dostoevsky a mere docetic or illusory appearance, but a real incarnation, which means that Christ felt the full range of human emotions, temptations, joys, and despair. When Dostoevsky insisted over and over that the Russian common people above all others had kept alive the image of Christ, he meant at least two things. First, no matter how shameful and base human beings become, the image of Christ can inspire them to seek forgiveness and to live a better life. Second, the image of Christ leads them to see hope in their own suffering for their sins and to long for moral transformation. Dostoevsky did not encourage his fellow believers to think that in doing evil they could escape the consequences of their deeds. Indeed, he insisted that freedom entails that the human actions carry consequences both for the doer of the deeds and for others. The innocent suffer along with the guilty.

Christ's suffering has, in Dostoevsky's theology, a profound "moral influence." Christ's entire life has become a moral influence for Christians everywhere. Even though Dostoevsky never fulfilled his dream of writing a book on Christ, enough is known of his view of Christ's sacrifice to allow us to conclude that it differs radically from that found in Augustine, Anselm, Luther, and Calvin. The model drawn from a legal or commercial exchange—of paying a ransom to either God or Satan—simply does not appear in Dostoevsky's theology. Christ's sacrifice is viewed as primarily his compassion to the point of becoming *involved* in human life with all its risks, contingencies, suffering, and death.[1]

In Chapter VII, we argued that Anselm's theory of atonement has deep roots in the classical Greek tragedies. The sacrifice somehow restores the objective moral order. We wish now to argue that whoever wishes to understand Dostoevsky's view of Christ's sacrificial life must see it in light of the classical Greek view of tragedy. Dostoevsky's interpretation of tragedy is, however, not Anselm's.

Drawing heavily from Aristotle's *Poetics*, Dorothea Krook in *Elements of Tragedy* contends that classical tragedy has four basic elements:

- The *act* (or series of acts) of *shame* or *horror* that precipitates the spectacle of suffering in the drama

---

[1]Given Dostoevsky's analysis of the human condition, it would seem to be impossible for any human being—including Christ—to reach adulthood without having become involved personally in doing harm to others. Strictly speaking, despite Alyosha's reference to Christ's blood as "innocent" (246; bk. 5, ch. 4), all persons are a part of original conflict and have the quality of naked consciousness. Dostoevsky's detailed Christology cannot be explored in this book. Edward Wasiolek's insight into Dostoevsky's dialectic of goodness and evil is in this connection, however, worth quoting:

> Not every character who does "good" in Dostoevsky's world is good, and not every character who does "evil" is evil. Unless we are ready to recognize the dialectical nature of the world, we shall continue to take love as love, when it may be hate as in *The Gambler*; sacrifice as sacrifice, when it may be insult as with Katerina in *The Brothers Karamazov*; suffering as suffering, where it may be willfulness and self-love as with the Underground Man. (Wasiolek 58)

- The *suffering* itself

- The *knowledge* and *insight* into the fundamental human condition—the insight that comes only through the process of suffering

- The *affirmation* or *reaffirmation* of human worth and dignity that emerges through great suffering and insight.

The worthwhileness of human life is discovered through insight into the agony created by violating the objective moral order and violating the dignity of others (Krook 8-17).

In high mimetic tragedy (e.g., *Oedipus Rex* and *King Lear*), the tragic hero "is all mankind: representative of all humanity" (Krook 36). Dostoevsky's Christ is the Second Adam, the Representative Man. In his detailed analysis of biblical texts on the atonement theme, John Driver describes the Representative Man in words that closely express Dostoevsky's image of Christ:

> Another strand of biblical thought which helps us to understand the identification of the Messiah with the peace which he brings is found in the archetypal images of Representative Man, which as we have already noted, was one of the ways in which the primitive community understood the meaning of the work of Christ. Christ creates "in himself one new man...so making peace" (Eph. 2:15). Jesus the Messiah in his life of total obedience to the Father even to the point of death was vindicated by God and glorified in the resurrection. Therefore it can be said that the righteousness of Jesus Christ, the Representative Man, leads to righteousness of life for all. (Rom. 5:18) (Driver 221)

Driver adds that the image of Christ as God in human form and as Representative Man enables the community of believers to see how the phrase "in himself" and "in one body" (Eph. 2:15-16) can be associated concretely with the messianic community, the church (cf. Eph. 1:23; I Cor. 12:27). "Jesus, who fulfilled the messianic mission of the Father, was representatively what the new

messianic people are called on to be" (Driver 221). It is in this context of the image of messianic "one body" that Dostoevsky challenges his readers in *The Diary of a Writer*: "Try to divide yourself; to determine where your personality ends and another personality begins.... For Christianity,...such a suggestion cannot even be put into words" (Ivanov 55).

Whereas Anselm and his heirs have emphasized the suffering of Christ as expiation and payment to God and his moral order, Dostoevsky views the suffering of Christ as God's love and forgiveness made manifest in his involvement in the community of human suffering. The image of Christ's life and suffering provides also inspiration for the sinner who suffers the slings and arrows of life and who struggles to resist the temptations. In this struggle, the sinner gains life.

It is important to understand, however, the model by which Dostoevsky's theology operates at this point. The sinner receives life from God. Nature and grace converge. The sinner encounters life's blessings by going on in the face of suffering. The insight or knowledge gained leads to the affirmation of human dignity within the messianic community and under the moral order established by God.

Dostoevsky did not imply that salvation as justification in God's eyes can be earned. In a sense, Dostoevsky was more Protestant than the Reformers themselves, for he started with divine grace and did not hold that a radical change in God had to be effected in order to elicit grace. According to Dostoevsky's theology, salvation is a process, a way of living, rather than a legal state of being.

One of the early steps in the salvation process is *forgiveness of oneself*. In *The Possessed*, Nikolai Stavrogin confesses to the kind Bishop Tikhon a horrible and shameful sin against the child Matryosha:

> "There is no forgiveness for me," Stavrogin said
> grimly. "It says in your book here that there's no greater crime
> than to offend 'one of these little ones,' and there can be none!"

The bishop, replying that he had good news for Stavrogin, adds:

"Christ will forgive you, too, if you succeed in forgiving
yourself—no, wait, don't listen to me; I was blaspheming: even
if you don't attain peace with yourself and fail to forgive
yourself, He will still forgive you for your intention and for your
great suffering...." (440; pt. 2, ch. 9)

The priority of divine grace and forgiveness is central to Dostoevsky's
theology. Christ forgives before sinners forgive themselves. Self-forgiveness
entails honest recognition and confession of the evil done. Stavrogin has not found
the peace of self-acceptance because he cannot *accept* forgiveness. And yet, the
bishop recognizes that Stavrogin has suffered a great deal, not as an atonement or
appeasement, but because he has grasped the shock and horror of his evil act and
because a war rages within him. In his attempt to face the consequences of evil
deeds, the process of tearing down the wall of hubris and confronting one's
wickedness comes only with great inner struggle and even agony. For
Dostoevsky, suffering is not a self-flagellation to earn merit, but the pain of
self-discovery and the pain of battle against one's own evil deeds and despair.

Bishop Tikhon says to Stavrogin, "You are longing for martyrdom and
self-sacrifice: well, overcome that desire too..." (*The Possessed* 441; pt. 2, ch. 9).
After encouraging him to overcome his pride, Tikhon urges him to go to a
monastery to learn from an old man with "Christian insight." Tikhon advises
Stavrogin—who has committed horrors and shameful deeds—to become a secret
novice. This is practical advice. Stavrogin's wickedness is deep-seated. It will
take years of struggle—great sacrifice—before goodness will have a fighting chance
in such a wicked heart. It is noteworthy that Tikhon recommends that Stavrogin
become, not a monk confined to the monastery, but a novice "living in the world"
(442; pt. 2, ch. 9).

Sadly, Stavrogin does not take the advice of the bishop-psychologist.
Instead, he leaves and then loses his battle with evil. In *The Brothers Karamazov*,
another young man, Alyosha, goes to an old man of Christian insight, Zosima, for
counsel and instruction. Alyosha the novice takes in effect the counsel of both
Bishop Tikhon and Elder Zosima by leaving the monastery to live as a man of
compassion and insight in a world of conflict and struggle against evil.

Christ the Hero

Aristotle's understanding of Greek tragedy included the courage of the hero who possesses "greatness of soul." Dostoevsky gives vital meaning to courage and bestows on it a new and positive status among the Christian virtues, just as Aristotle before him made courage the defining virtue of the "Magnanimous Man" in his *Nicomachean Ethics* (Krook 53). In Dostoevsky's theology, Christ is not only "greatness of soul" incarnate, but also for believers the hero whose courage in the face of hardship and suffering inspires them to struggle daily against despair and temptation.

Dostoevsky's Christ sacrificed by choosing to become human and thereby to suffer for all, just as all human beings suffer for all. In *Crime and Punishment,* Sonya chooses to sacrifice herself for others, not as a masochistic venture, but to save her family. She has the choice of walking away from her family and leaving them to their own miserable end. Instead, she becomes a prostitute in order to rescue her parents, brothers and sisters from starvation. She becomes a woman of sin so that others might live.

Chapter X. The Double Incarnate

Dostoevsky's Book about Christ

On December 24, 1877, Dostoevsky at the age of fifty-six set forth in "Memento for My Whole Life" his plans for the next ten years of his life. Among them was the plan to "write a book about Jesus Christ" (Krag 290). He lived only three years and one month of those ten years. What might he have said about Jesus; and why did this celebrated novelist desire to write about him? A part of the answer goes back to his years in the Siberian prison, where he felt alienated even from his fellow prisoners. The image or ideal of Christ became exceedingly important in helping him through the ordeal of Siberian misery. At the age of thirty-two, he wrote to a friend that Christ symbolized for him everything beautiful or lovely, profound, sympathetic, reasonable, courageous, and perfect ("To Mme. N. D. Fonvisin" 71). Unquestionably, the image of Christ had a deep moral and emotional hold on him. Over the next quarter of a century, he doubtless modified it in some of the details, but it remained central to him personally and to his fundamental view of the world.

Dostoevsky had read books that portrayed the life of Jesus without the miracles. His contemporaries Ernest Renan and David Friedrich Strauss, nineteenth-century historians and biblical scholars, had portrayed Jesus as something of a humanist liberal (Renan 33, 136). Strauss in particular regarded the Fourth Gospel to be unreliable as a historical document and thought that the other three Gospels contained considerable "myth" (Strauss 53-4; Robinson 55-6). Dostoevsky knew of the belief of some biblical scholars and historians that Jesus' prediction of the Kingdom's arrival at a particular time and place had simply failed to materialize, thus making Jesus quite fallible about at least one element of his message and mission (Sullivan 54-63).

Dostoevsky's own notion of the "Russian Christ," which he never spelled out in his novels, intertwined with his view that the Russian peasants of the Orthodox Church embodied the spirit of Christ in a special way. Dostoevsky believed that both Christ and the Russian people had sacrificed and suffered much, and there is reason to think that he thought of Christ as at least the tragic savior-hero who endured great agony and humiliation.

The Temptation of Christ

"The Legend of the Grand Inquisitor" offers evidence that Dostoevsky, like Strauss, spent considerable time in thinking about the temptations of Christ. In speculating about what Dostoevsky would have written in a book about Christ, we would do well to remind ourselves that, for Dostoevsky, to complete a book was more than writing it. It was research. And above all, it was an intellectual, moral, and emotional adventure. In addition, writing a book on Christ would have involved a personal risk for Dostoevsky. In probing the meaning of the temptations, for example, he would sooner or later have been forced to ask the question of the reality of the temptations. Were they mere play-acting? Was it a forgone conclusion that Jesus would not yield to any temptations?

As a literary artists and a life-long explorer of the human heart, Dostoevsky could scarcely conclude that Christ's temptations were unreal, a pretense and deception. At the same time, if Jesus Christ truly might have sinned, the orthodox Christian is faced with the unnerving question as to whether the Second Person of the Godhead would have incurred guilt, not second-hand guilt as if he were taking on the debt of someone else, but direct personal guilt because of his own involvement in evildoing? Would "the sinless One" who came to be the Savior have lost his capacity to be the Savior? Or by carrying out the premises of his view of original conflict and inevitable sin, would Dostoevsky have concluded that Christ's true sacrifice was that of becoming sinful by participating literally in the inevitable sin of the human race?

If the Christ portrayed in "The Legend of the Grand Inquisitor" closely resembles Dostoevsky's own image of Christ, then Christ in the temptations faced genuine risk. Otherwise, Christ would have lacked free will, which in Dostoevsky's thought is the essential quality of being human. It follows, then, that in appearing on earth as a human being, Dostoevsky's Christ might have sinned grievously.[1]

The question about Christ's sinning is not wild speculation. According to Dostoevsky's own views, original and inevitable conflict, when combined with human fallibility, virtually guarantees that each individual will yield to some temptation or do harm to others. Indeed, in some passages of Matthew, Jesus appears rather vicious, using words like "fools," "serpents," and "vipers" to refer to other human beings. His talk of casting sinners into a "furnace of fire" (Mt. 13:42) or into "outer darkness" where they will weep and gnash their teeth (Mt. 8:12) scarcely exemplifies the Golden Rule.

Prince Myshkin of *The Idiot*, the character dearest to Dostoevsky's heart, proved to be his most difficult character to create. Novelists find it much more difficult to write about a truly good person than to write about either an evil person or one who is an ordinary mixture of good and evil. Dostoevsky told his niece, to whom he promised to dedicate the novel, that it was "infinitely difficult" to capture Absolute Beauty (i.e., loveliness and goodness) in writing and went on to speak of Christ as "the infinitely lovely figure" ("To His Niece" 142). Myshkin, a kind of Christ-like individual, represents Dostoevsky's own painful struggle to come to terms with a realistic image of Christ.

---

[1]This poses for orthodoxy a serious question of divine foreknowledge. If the Godhead had foreknown that Jesus would sin if he should come to earth as a human being, would the Godhead have sent him nevertheless? Or would the plan have been set aside in deference to another plan? If the answer to the latter question is *Yes*, then the question emerges as to why the Adam-and-Eve plan had not been replaced by a better one?

The Great Challenge

Mochulsky, in his splendid study of Dostoevsky's life and works, contends that Dostoevsky overcame his temptation to write a "novel about Christ" (350). We suggest, however, that Dostoevsky more than likely did not venture it because he sensed that he was not ready. In the process of writing *The Idiot*, he must have realized that writing a novel about Christ could be the most arduous task of his life.

We suggest that at least two other factors would have made writing a book about Christ Dostoevsky's greatest challenge:

- First, as a skilled adapter of the literary works of others, Dostoevsky might well have come to see that the Gospel writers in the New Testament had taken a number of stories from the Old Testament and adapted them for their own purposes. The feeding of the five thousand, the raising of the daughter, and the cursing of the fig tree are only the beginning of the adaptations (Helms). In fact, Dostoevsky knew that David Friedrich Strauss had already argued that the Gospel composers had raided the Hebrew Bible for stories and details about the putative life of Jesus.[1] Dostoevsky would therefore have had to work through the problem of the authenticity of the Gospels.

- Second, assuming that Dostoevsky would have devoted as much research and thought to writing the book on Jesus as he had devoted to writing *Crime and Punishment*, *The Possessed*, or *A Raw Youth*, he could not have settled for either the superficial "harmony of the Gospels" that some orthodox Christians had put

---

[1]The English novelist George Eliot, Dostoevsky's contemporary, translated Strauss' *Das Leben Jesu* into English.

forth or what New Testament scholar F. C. Burkitt called a "a simple series of disconnected anecdotes" (Schweitzer xviii). But if he could settle for neither of these two alternatives, he would have had to construct an image of Jesus by somehow working afresh through the Gospel constructions and inventions. (Wells 1-10)

Myshkin of *The Idiot* and the Christ of "The Legend of the Grand Inquisitor" provide clues as to how Dostoevsky's research on and construction of his life of Christ might have begun. How the portrayal would have developed in full must remain, of course, a matter of conjecture. In some ways, the various "lives of Jesus" composed over the years, including orthodox Christianity's imagined harmony of the Gospels, resemble more the diverse readings of a Rorschach test than the accounts of modern biographies or thoroughly researched historical novels.[1]

A Christian Tragedy

Mochulsky states outright that "a novel about Christ is impossible," but he does not clarify the reasons behind his statement (346). Michael Holquist comes close to saying—without putting it clearly in words—that although someone could write a novel about the human Jesus Christ, no one could write a novel or novel-biography of God on earth (111). Strauss criticizes the "artless supernatural way of regarding the life of Jesus" (Zahrnt 41). The Second Person of the Godhead doubtless could not serve as the hero of a novel if being God entails having no character growth, taking no real risks, and having no past or future (Talbert 2).

Dostoevsky's God is not, however, Aristotle's Unmoved Mover uninvolved in human affairs. One of the limitations of Myshkin as a human being, we suggest, is that Dostoevsky did not allow him to become *actively* involved. He is too passive to be a full human being, and yet the all-too-human characters in

---

[1]In his Harvard University dissertation, Richard I. Pervo contends that the Acts of the Apostles is an adventure novel (Pervo).

The Idiot react to Myshkin so that his impact on them is so real as to be almost overwhelming. Ironically, Myshkin's impact leads to great harm and evil.

In Myshkin's impact, we come face to face with the truth of Dostoevsky's doctrine of original conflict, for even in his passive innocence Myshkin is *inescapably involved*. In some respects, he is not *of* the world. But in other respects, he is *in* it, shining in his beauty and goodness, while both generating great evil and suffering great evil. We insist that Dostoevsky experimented with Myshkin, using him as the stalking horse of the Christ figure, allowing him to substitute for Christ to see how goodness or Absolute Beauty might fare in the world of sinners and sinful believers.

There is perhaps still another reason that Dostoevsky at the age of fifty-six had yet to write a novel about Jesus. As a Christian artist, he doubtless realized that it would be for him the supreme challenge to enter into the subjective states of Christ, seeing the world from Christ"s point of view, reporting Christ's secret thought, divulging his doubts, and exposing to light his fallible judgments and his human urges. Dostoevsky as a novelist simply could not have forsworn probing deeply into the character, conflicts, and human personality of Jesus (Culpepper 105, 110).

According to orthodox Christian theology of the East and the West, Christ was both fully God and fully Man. Despite the fact that throughout his literary career Dostoevsky seemed almost preoccupied with the theme of "the double," he, the great Russian novelist, could not have written a novel about the God-Man in which *both* faces of "the double" come to life. This does not imply a limitation on Dostoevsky's artistic talent, however, since the Gospel writers themselves do not succeed in revealing the inner life of the deity in whom they profess to believe.

New Testament scholars today acknowledge that not one of the four Gospels provides a biography of a person named Jesus (Moore). Each Gospel is more a theological work than a historical account or a biography in the modern sense (Talbert 1-17). The Gospels do not explore with any profundity the cognitive limitations of the Jesus figure because of the authors' need to give him divinity. The same need also seems to have prevented the authors from providing any insight into Christ's sexuality. The Gospels contain much about the "role" of Jesus, but they provide little in-depth probing into his inner personality.

Despite this fact, however, more than enough material exists in the Gospels to serve the purpose of a truly creative novelist. Current literary criticism tends to treat the Gospels themselves more as stories of faith than as historical accounts. Even if none of the four Gospels qualifies as a tragedy, a sensitive novelist could weave together threads and strands in the Gospel to make a profound and moving tragedy.

According to Matthew 27:46 and Mark 15:34, Jesus cried with a loud voice, "My God, my God, why hast thou forsaken me?" Dorothea Krook, raising the question of the meaning of *why* in this passage, suggests that Christ from the cross did not know what *purpose* or *end* his dying in such agony and degradation served. It was a bitter, anguished cry. We suggest that Ivan's bitter protest in the tavern raises precisely the same question. For what purpose or end is all the human suffering and agony? Through Ivan, Dostoevsky succeeds in exploring in his last novel some of the basic elements of the tragedy. Ten years earlier in *The Idiot*, he had written a complete tragedy about, ironically, an innocent Christ-like person.

Myshkin and Original Conflict

Despite Dostoevsky's Herculean efforts, Myshkin never becomes fully human. He resembles the Christ of the docetics, who taught that Christ merely seemed to have a body and its passions. Despite what orthodox theologians claim, the Gospel writers themselves never succeeded in fully overcoming the docetic habit. The Christ of the Gospels is not wholly incarnate, perhaps because the attempt to become Universal Mankind (to say nothing of becoming fully divine and fully human) eventually reaches a point of diminishing returns. The "synthesis" loses its individuality. While people react to Myshkin, he appears in his story as a rather passive person drained of a truly adult personality. Mochulsky contends that Myshkin's "divine character" has disappeared (350). We claim that his human character never comes fully into being because in some respects Myshkin remains in the story a child who cannot enter adulthood. His incarnation is therefore incomplete. The reason that Myshkin persisted as an enigma for Dostoevsky lies in the basic aloofness of the character from human reality. By contrast, the novel's other characters, sometimes shockingly real, form a more chilling and tragic world than that of *Crime and Punishment*.

Had Dostoevsky attempted a novel about Christ, he would have had to deal concretely with the question of whether a human being living in a world of other human beings can live without committing sin and bringing some pain and harm to others. Myshkin, sinless in an abstract sense, unquestionably contributes to enormous harm and suffering for others.[1] Even he could not escape becoming a part of the original conflict and inevitable evil.

---

[1]Even Sonya, whom Charles Passage describes as the wholly passive Madonna ideal embodying the principle of Good, is a prostitute (142-3). The good individuals of three of Dostoevsky's classics—Alyosha, Myshkin, and Sonya—function in many ways as prism personalities. Regarding the novelist's problem of making good characters interesting, Dostoevsky's remark about the republicans, the heroes of *Les Miserables*, is noteworthy. He calls them ridiculous, puffed up, and implausible figures. "His [Hugo's] villains are far better. Where these fallen people are real, on Victor Hugo's part, there are always humaneness, love, and magnanimity..." (Belknap, *The Genesis* 39).

Chapter XI. Theodicy and the Divine Abyss

The Question of Immortality

Theodicy, a branch of philosophical theology, struggles to harmonize the facts of evil and suffering with the theological premise that the Creator is both the governor of the universe and the supreme exemplification of love. If the Creator is regarded as omnipotent, omniscient and omnipresent, the problem of harmonizing becomes so severe that some writers have declared it beyond solution.

If the Creator were not loving, the theological problem of evil would no longer exist. Dostoevsky does not take this route out of the difficulty, however, for the plain reason that a loveless Creator would not be God. For Dostoevsky, creation itself would be bleak indeed if love were cut off at the Source. He views life in its finite manifestations as the overflow of divine love. The love of life that resounds in Dostoevsky's novels would be inconceivable if divine love had not initiated life at the finite level. Dostoevsky seems to think that life and love are so intricately bound that even if life could come into existence without love, it could not thrive. This is perhaps a way of saying that elemental love *is* life caring

for itself. Infinite love, then, for Dostoevsky, lies behind every manifestation of life.

Dostoevsky couples belief in God with belief in immortality. At first glance, this link might appear to be based on the simple view that the practice of virtue requires life after death. Virtuous human mortals would receive rewards and the wicked would receive just punishment that the temporal, terrestrial life had not provided consistently. While this simple view is an ingredient of Dostoevsky's theodicy, it cannot be for him the whole story. Since Dostoevsky's God is not the bookkeeper that some medieval preachers envisioned, the question of sorting out eternal rewards to the deserving individuals is misconceived.

Why then does the great Russian novelist seem preoccupied with immortality if he does not view life after death as the time of reckoning in accord with the debits and credits of the heavenly Bookkeeper? The answer is that Dostoevsky is preoccupied with life, with the process of living to the fullest. Without immortality, he believes, the initial divine investment in life comes to nothing. God is love just because he cares for life. The termination of life is the termination of love, and Dostoevsky regards such a termination as a defeat for the God who is love. God loses if his human creatures, who can love consciously and voluntarily, come into the world only to be snuffed out permanently.

Dostoevsky's God is not Aristotle's Unmoved Mover who experiences no care for the world. The Eastern Church that nurtured Dostoevsky draws heavily upon the Gospel of John and the Johannine Epistles, which stress the theme "God is love"
(I John 4:8). For Dostoevsky, since love entails caring, God, who is the supreme exemplification of love, cannot turn his back on his human creatures once he has brought them into being. If God as Mother Earth brings human beings into existence and infuses them with life, then she cannot abandon her children by reducing them to oblivion.

The theme of immortality in Dostoevsky's novels turns out to be entwined with the complex question of meaning. Dostoevsky is indisputably a teleologist. His God provides a meaning or purpose to creation simply by creating life. That is, *the purpose and meaning of life is life itself,* a point on which Ivan and Alyosha seem to agree when they, sitting in the tavern, face the issue of theodicy.

The Challenge of Ivan

Ivan argued earlier, at the monastery, that human beings require belief in immortality if they are to go on living. At first glance, Ivan's argument seems to be that if human beings do not believe in immortality, they will relate to one another as reptiles ready to devour their prey. At a deeper level, however, Ivan seems to assume that if people do not believe in immortality, they will quickly see no point in loving, honoring, and respecting each other. If love is soon done for, and if life along with love is quickly extinguished, why care for life and other human beings?

Ivan makes it clear that to have life is to cherish it (230-1; bk. 5, ch. 3). This is a profound insight, for it implies that love in the sense of caring and cherishing is already built into life. Ivan does not come to cherish and care for certain experiences and relationships because he has deduced from prior premises that he ought to do so. Rather, he *discovers* that he has this caring and cherishing as a part of himself as a living human being. The only question is whether the love (as caring and cherishing) within him will remain alive after he reaches the age of thirty (230; bk. 5 ch. 3). But why should it perish after thirty years? While not directly answering the question in *The Brothers Karamazov*, Dostoevsky does imply the following answer. As Ivan grows older, the impact of believing in his own permanent extinction will eventually rob him of his courage. The specter of death will chill the natural love that has sprung up in his heart from Mother Earth. In short, a kind of grieving will begin to settle in and turn his love into bitterness. Already, Ivan shows signs of the struggle between love and bitterness. He becomes intensely fond of his younger brother (234; bk. 5, ch. 3), but later in the novel he turns cold toward him (601-2; bk. 11, ch. 5). A conspicuous war rages inside Ivan regarding his brothers Dmitri and Alyosha, a war between natural warmth and affection, on the one hand, and peevishness and hostility, on the other hand (652-5; bk. 11, ch. 10).

The romantic involvements in the Karamazov story, far from serving as mere entertainment and sparkle, prove essential to the basic theme of this searching philosophical novel. The romantic involvements of the Karamazovs *are* life and love in action. They are love itself emerging sometimes painfully and impulsively, but unfailingly. Ivan finds himself loving because, in part, he has found himself *in love* (232; bk. 5, ch. 3). And yet, Dostoevsky does not cheat in exploring the theme of theodicy. He portrays love itself, and therefore life, as

complicated, entangled, and filled with almost unbearable anguish and turmoil. It is as if for Dostoevsky only the novel could serve as the medium through which to communicate the raging conflicts of life and love. Ivan has insisted that at least some of the conflicts are so outrageous that even if there were a grand "harmony" in the next life, in the glorious future, it would not justify the horrors and sufferings of terrestrial existence (236; bk. 5, ch. 3).

In *The Possessed*, a slashing novel of political philosophy, Dostoevsky earlier attacked the utopians who would bring about great slaughter, arson, and agony in service of the glorious future that some of the socialists and communists had proposed. Ironically, Ivan Karamazov seems to take the most powerful arguments from *The Possessed* so that he may turn them with a vengeance against the theodicy of Dostoevsky's own Christian tradition. The relentless savagery of the attack in *The Possessed* becomes no less savage in the mouth of Ivan in *The Brothers Karamazov*. Only a novelist and philosopher of the genius and courage to equal Dostoevsky's could turn his own arguments so forcefully against his own basic convictions.

It may be asked how a writer like Dostoevsky could turn upon his beloved Orthodox theology with such fury and relentless criticism. We offer the hypothesis that Dostoevsky's philosophical theology contained all the ingredients that made it possible for him to advance a new solution to the problem of evil and suffering, a solution that moves beyond the camp of classical theodicy. To do elementary justice to Dostoevsky's theodicy, however, we must cast it in historical perspective.

Ultimate Dualism

Before becoming a Christian, Augustine had struggled with the issue of theodicy. At one stage in his life, he embraced Manichee dualism, which has roots in the dualism of the Zoroastrianism that perhaps flourished in Persia during the reign of Darius (522-486 B.C.E.). Some biblical scholars hold that Zoroastrian dualism influenced the Hebrew religion and early Christianity (Snaith 95).

According to Zoroastrian teaching, two Spirits emanating from the Creator or Wise Lord carry on a perpetual battle with one another. The Evil spirit has several names, including Angra Mainyu and Shaitin or Satan. Zoroastrianism may have been the first religion to develop a full scheme of demonology whose

function was that of opposing goodness and spreading disease, death, and wrath. In the third century C.E., Zoroastrianism experienced a resurgence.

Augustine embraced for awhile a dualistic religion called Manichaeism that began perhaps in the third century by a Persian named Mani (215-276 C.E.). Its dualism, more pronounced than Zoroastrianism's, combined elements of Buddhism, Judaism, Christianity, and Zoroastrianism. According to Manichaeism, two ultimate forces or principles—Light and Darkness or God and Matter—make perpetual war on one another. Unlike Zoroaster, Mani insisted that God and Matter are not emanations of a higher God, but are coeternal and independent of each other. Far from being governed by one supreme deity, the universe reflects the ultimate dualism and conflict of Light versus Darkness, neither of whom created the other. Reconciliation between them, Mani thought, is impossible.

The theme of Light warring with Darkness appears in the Gospel of John. The Christian author of Ephesians spoke of the rulers of the "present darkness" (6:12). The Apostle Paul believed that he could foresee a time when God in Christ would triumph over all the evil principalities and powers (Phil. 2:9; Rom. 8:38-9).

Dostoevsky's novels portray a kind of dualism or warfare, God and the Devil at war within each individual person. Dostoevsky's view of the Devil and demons is not, however, easy to formulate into a coherent and systematic pattern. It is difficult to avoid concluding that Dostoevsky knowingly teased his readers and refused to set forth explicitly his view of demons and Satan. *The Possessed* is often translated *The Devils* and is prefaced with a quotation from Luke 8:32-7, which is about an exorcism.

An unrivaled work of art, the passage that describes Ivan's conversation with Satan leaves the reader unable to draw a definite conclusion as to whether the novel's narrator regards the supernatural visitor to be an actual being or a mutation within Ivan's subjectivity. Dostoevsky toys with the reader by allowing Ivan to raise the question as to whether the visitor is not simply Ivan himself. If the visitor has objective status, then Dostoevsky advances a kind of limited dualism of cosmic proportion. It is limited in that the Devil and his assistants will eventually come fully under the Creator's control—at least according to Eastern Orthodoxy. If the supernatural visitor is, however, Ivan's own involuntary creation or projection, the dualism lies in the human heart.

Dostoevsky's preoccupation with the idea of *the double in both The Idiot* and the novella *The Double* gives some support to the conjecture that his real

concern was to explore the duality of human personality. The sinister theme of multiple personality or at least altered states of consciousness plays so hauntingly and persistently in the background of all four of Dostoevsky's great novels that the careful reader cannot help wondering about the ontological status of duality. Some commentators have not hesitated, however, to conclude (or presuppose) that Dostoevsky takes seriously the objective reality of a cosmic Satan and cosmic demons (Terras, *Companion* 53, 353, 391). Later, we will suggest another way of interpreting Dostoevsky's long-term flirtation with metaphysical dualism.

Plato and Philo

A look at the theodicy of Philo and Plato can help elucidate Dostoevsky's theodicy. Philo Judaeus of Alexandria (fl. 20 B.C.E.—40 C.E.), one of the most rigorous theologians of antiquity, is the forerunner of later Jewish and Christian theologians. An older contemporary of the Apostle Paul, Philo tried to set forth a systematic doctrine of God derived, he believed, from the writings of Moses. At the same time, he tried to reconcile his Hebrew monotheism with the view of God found in Plato's astounding work *Timaeus*.

Before either the birth of Philo or the emergence of Christianity, Plato had contended that God could not be the author of evil. In *Timaeus,* Plato advances the idea that a kind of primordial matter exists eternally alongside God. In addition, there exists, according to *Timaeus*, a realm of eternal ideas or norms that God did not create. God, serving as the Great Architect or Demiurge, took the formless matter, informed or shaped it, and, using the realm of ideas to guide his creative work, transformed the shapeless chaos into cosmos or an orderly world. Philo, while holding Plato in high esteem, could not as a Jew bring himself to postulate that either the realm of ideas or the formless matter could exist eternally alongside God prior to the creation of the world. Having labored to reconcile inconsistencies in the Hebrew scriptures, Philo resolved to reconcile his Hebrew tradition with Plato.

Before examining Philo's attempted reconciliation, we must point out that the problem of theodicy does not plague the theology of *Timaeus* in the way that it plagues Jewish and Christian theologies, including the Hebrew drama of Job and his suffering. For Plato in *Timaeus*, God's creative work begins with a *given*, namely, shapeless motion or matter. This given supplies the Great Architect with both potentiality and limitations as to what can be created.

Philo, unable to accept the Platonic hypothesis that other realities could exist eternally with God, revised Plato by conjecturing that God created primordial matter out of nothing. Next, from this primordial matter, God created the world. Presumably, the primordial matter gave God both potentiality and limitation for his second creation, the creation of the world.

The realm of ideas, according to *Timaeus*, exists co-eternal with God. Philo attempted to deal with the realm of eternal ideas by treating them as eternal thoughts residing inside the mind of God. They are eternal just because God's mind and its contents are eternal. Prior to creating the world, Philo's God created a duplicate of his ideas or thoughts and gave them a kind of external reality in the way that a builder might project from his mind the blueprints of his future work. Using both these projected ideas and the created matter, Philo's God then shaped the world into being.

In attempting to understand Dostoevsky's theodicy, readers of his novels may recall that Eastern Orthodoxy postulated an intimacy between the Creator and creation that made many Western Church theologians uneasy. There is no indication that Dostoevsky took the route of Plato and Philo by embracing an intermediatory matter that stood between the Creator and creation. Dostoevsky's personalism does not require this added step. And yet it cannot be denied that because of its limitations on the Creator's power, the intermediatory matter offers at least one possible explanation of the presence of evil and suffering in the world. Although Dostoevsky does not follow Plato and Philo at this point, it will be useful to keep their views of pre-existing matter in mind when trying to understand Dostoevsky's way of explaining evil and suffering.

John Milton's Theodicy

The English poet and essayist John Milton (1608-1674) is perhaps best known for his *Paradise Lost*, a sweeping Puritan theodicy. In it, the cosmic adversary of God brings sin to earth by means of successfully tempting Eve and Adam to disobey God's prohibition. More interesting and fruitful, however, is Milton's treatment of sin's emergence inside heaven itself. His great epic presupposes but does not clarify the *metaphysical possibility* of a revolt against God by the angels. According to the traditional theology of Eastern Orthodoxy, Roman Catholicism and Protestantism, upon entering heaven Christians will never have to face the real option of losing their newly secured position. For them, the

possibility of losing salvation and being damned will never again arise. The angels in heaven, however, having no such security, faced the possibility of succumbing to a revolt and ending up in everlasting hell.

Dostoevsky in his theodicy does not draw upon the Satan hypothesis to account for evil and suffering in the world. He perhaps understood that it not only failed to strike at the heart of the theodicy question, but added to or underscored more fundamental questions. How could a revolt have been staged inside heaven? Was there jealousy in heaven? Envy? Resentment? In short, *if the angels in heaven were and are in conflict, does that imply that original conflict exists inside heaven? Does conflict have some kind of metaphysical or ontological status inside the life of the Creator?*

As Christian theologians, both Milton and Dostoevsky had to deal with the question of the beginning of evil. Did evil somehow come into existence behind God's back? Did the Creator bring it about unwittingly? Could she or he have prevented it? Did the Creator foresee the consequences of giving a place to evil in the universe? Did God create from scratch? Or did she or he have to work with flawed raw material?

Milton rejected the orthodox doctrine of creation out of nothing (*ex nihilo*). He believed that the first chapter of Genesis and other creation passages in Scripture allow only the conclusion that God created the world out of pre-existing matter. Unlike Philo, Milton considered the creation of anything *ex nihilo* to be contrary to both Scripture and reason. Since the primordial matter had no existence independent of God, it had to proceed flawlessly from God. In short, matter was produced not out of nothing but out of God. This means that *God produced everything out of himself* (Conklin 71-3; Milton 919-1076).

Having drawn what he believed was a strictly scriptural conclusion, Milton went on to contend that since everything is created out of God, no created thing can be utterly annihilated (Conklin 72). Dostoevsky's doctrine of immortality may very well follow a train of thought similar to Milton's at this point, although Dostoevsky appears to have held that it was undying, loving energy rather than matter that proceeded from God and formed his new creatures. Creation is, for Dostoevsky, first and foremost divine love generating new centers of endless love out of his own life and love.

With life and love, however, comes conflict, Dostoevsky always believed. All his novels portray love in conflict. As noted in Chapter III, for Dostoevsky earthly paradise exists in conflict, love, and forgiveness. The question remains,

then, as to *whether original conflict exists in the heavenly paradise, in the life of the God of love.*

E. S. Brightman's Personalism

During the years in which Dostoevsky was writing *A Raw Youth, The Possessed* and *The Brothers Karamazov,* Borden Parker Bowne systematically formulated the metaphysics of personalism. In so doing, he not only portrayed nature as God's own energizing, but wrote compellingly of the emergence of multiple centers of consciousness. For Bowne, evolution is the process by which God's energy gives birth to diverse and numerous selves and persons whose consciousness, while dependent upon God, is distinct from the divine consciousness. In the early 1930s, Bowne's most original and promising student E. S. Brightman struggled with the fact that Bowne's personalism failed to deal adequately with the problems of time, evil, and suffering. With characteristic boldness and philosophic acumen, Brightman reformulated Bowne's doctrine of God by contending that the conflict in nature profoundly reflected conflict within the life of God.

Like Dostoevsky, Brightman had studied Voltaire's *Candide* as well as other attempts to demonstrate that traditional Christian theodicies had failed to make a case for a loving, omnipotent, and omniscient Providence. Convinced that personalism offered the most comprehensive and coherent philosophical perspective, Brightman amended Bowne's personalism for the purpose of making it both more coherent and empirically sensitive to the suffering and evil in the world. He agreed that the God of Bowne was indeed the Cosmic Person. Brightman went further, however, to add that as the supreme exemplification of personhood, God, far from being a static or timeless Being, lives a life of dynamic interaction with the selves and persons that emerge out of his ceaseless energy.

While Bowne perhaps implied that God experienced inner process, he never made it explicit and seemed to have serious reservations about making God temporal in any fundamental sense. Brightman, by contrast, boldly renounced the view of God as timeless eternity and began to speak of the Cosmic Person as *omnitemporal.* Although having neither beginning nor end, Brightman's God takes on new experiences perpetually. Clearly, Brightman broke with the classical theistic perspective that, despite numerous attempts to conceive of God as

genuinely personal, seemed always to fall back on a God who in some mysterious way had already lived his/her life.

Contrary to classical theism, Brightman's God has a future just because divine love and creativity require a future. According to classical theism, God has in some sense already solved all problems, reached all the conclusions that can ever be drawn, and has total and irrevocable comprehension of everything that ever will be. Strictly speaking, the God of classical theism has neither past nor future but is one eternal Now. Traditionally, classical theists have tried to portray God as both affected and unaffected by the world. They have viewed time as both real and unreal for God, who presumably relates intimately to the temporal events of creation and yet is unrelated and entirely nontemporal. The Calvinists among classical theists went so far as to conclude that the Creator not only foreknows everything but is the primary cause in bringing about every good deed and every evil deed in the universe.

Brightman came to believe that classical theism and Calvinism in particular played fast and loose with the phenomenon of time. John Milton's contemporary philosopher Baruch Spinoza (1632-1677) took Calvinism to its logical conclusion by declaring time to be an illusion of the finite mind. Modern Calvinists, continuing to hold that time is both real and illusory, portray the Creator as temporarily going along with finite mortals in their illusion. Indeed, this divine pretense becomes a part of the doctrine of Christ's incarnation.

Unwilling to jump back and forth between taking time as real and taking it as unreal, Brightman postulated that God as the Cosmic Person truly does both live and interact (rather than pretending to interact) with those finite centers of consciousness that evolve out of his own consciousness or energizing. In short, living and interacting in love require *time and process even for God*.

Once he took a route that veered away from classical theism and Calvinism in particular, Brightman did not fail to make explicit what was implicit in his new venture. If time and process are truly real for the Cosmic Person, then God has a future that is more than a formal deduction from his/her past and present. God literally experiences novelty and cannot unfailingly predict or infallibly foreknow every event of the future. The future is not an actual reality even for God, although God's past and present form to some extent the ground of potentiality and limitation for the future.

Dostoevsky's novels offer no suggestion that he believed in divine predestination. Nor do they suggest that he held that God knows infallibly all the future. This does not prove that Dostoevsky consciously gave up the doctrine of divine omniscience. Radical human freedom and free will are, however, so central to his paradigm that predestination could never be reconciled to it. Some classical theists concede that they have never encountered a successful reconciliation between human freedom and the infallible foreknowledge traditionally attributed to the deity. Brightman not only came to view infallible foreknowledge as an impossibility, but also set out to build the case that the widespread suffering and evil (both natural and moral evil) in the world cannot be adequately explained apart from the hypothesis that *the Creator harbors original conflict*.

Dostoevsky's novels do not provide a systematic theology and theodicy. They contain, however, enough material about the nature of love to allow the tentative conjecture that if Dostoevsky's vision of God were set forth as a systematic and coherent whole, it would include in the divine life a conflict or struggle that is peculiar to life and vital love. Augustine wrote of the restless human heart, but Dostoevsky's novels suggest a restlessness in love itself. Granted, we are trying to speak systematically whereas Dostoevsky wrote his theodicy in story form. But it is difficult to think of conscious life—including the divine consciousness—as Dostoevsky conceived of it without including in it both *agape* and restless *eros*.

If Aristotle's God is the Unmoved Mover, the God of Dostoevsky and Brightman is the Self-moved Mover. At the inner heart of God is the everlasting will or desire (*eros*) to create values and to let the divine love (*agape*) overflow and reproduce itself in finite selves and persons. Brightman referred to the divine restlessness or surging energy as the *nonrational Given*, which with the *rational Given* (the eternal norms) sustains in the divine nature a perpetual polarity. For Brightman, much suffering and evil in the world comes because human beings both voluntarily and involuntarily violate one another in numerous ways. Not all evil and suffering, however, can be accounted for in this way. The Cosmic Person's nonrational Given perpetually generates not only great values but also severe conflict that often leads to suffering, agony, and death. Indeed, Brightman does not turn away from stating that the world contains "surd evil" that cannot be harmonized with perfect goodness (Brightman 246, 333). The tragic dimension to God's nature overflows into nature and human life. God is perfect will-to-value, Brightman argues, but the divine nonrational Given surges with such abundant life that it cannot be brought into full control of the rational Given. It

is as if the divine *eros* or energy moves out in so many directions that complete control of it is impossible.

There is perhaps no more accurate way to describe the nonrational Given of Brightman's God than to say that God's infinite potentiality or creativity comes perpetually in conflict with itself. Nature, surging with life, is also blood red in tooth and claw. Human beings, emerging in the image of the Cosmic Person, experience both self-conflict and conflict with others while at the same time loving and living as creators of values.

Augustine and Negation

We offer the hypothesis that Dostoevsky's understanding of evil was far more profound than Augustine's. Augustine imported some of his Neoplatonism into Christianity when he conceived of evil as estranged being void of goodness. In his insightful study *Augustine on Evil*, G. R. Evans concludes that while the problem of evil plagued Augustine for many years, he eventually came to identify evil as nothing real (149). Like Anselm of Bec, Augustine found it difficult to discuss coherently something (evil) that does not exist. He gave it, therefore, a kind of existence as a negation of being and goodness (Evans 175). The problem of evil became a dilemma for Augustine. Either evil was actual and real or it was void of actuality and therefore unreal. If it was possessed of actuality, then Manichean dualism gained credibility. If evil was not real, then what is salvation all about and why does the appearance of evil in everyday life persist with such strength?

Dostoevsky, as early as his *Notes from Underground*, came to view evil as the opposite of love and involved living. The anti-hero in *Notes* satirizes those who, Dostoevsky believed, would hang life and human commitment with the rope of pseudo-rationality. The thrust of *Notes* is that existence means vital involvements and commitments. Evil is the loss of meaning in the sense of trying to live without commitments and personal involvements. Nihilism is, quite simply, the negation of life as reaching out and becoming a part of the process of human interaction and the risk of commitment. The anti-hero of *Notes* is a "sick man" in that he drains himself of life and love. He is a man in process of becoming demonic, which is life turning on itself in resentment and spite.

Throughout Dostoevsky's novels, but especially in *The Possessed* (sometimes translated **The Devils**), Dostoevsky leaves clues as to what he takes the

demonic to be. It is everything that tempts or pulls the individual from engagement with life and love. In *The Possessed*, Nikolai Vsevolodovich Stavrogin looms almost as omnipresent evil. The evil of Nikolai is that of not caring, of not being involved and committed. Nothing really matters to him. The "problem" of Nikolai in the novel has to do with whether this walking death—whose face is like a mask—will come to life. Will Nikolai turn into a committed, involved, loving human being who, forsaking his deadly indifference, learns to care for himself and others? Or will he remain the specter of someone who both is and is not human?

We will not go into the question of whether Nikolai—whom Dostoevsky's narrator calls Prince Hal (Shakespeare's experiment with a dual personality)—is a dual person. Rather, we call attention to the fact that it is in *The Possessed* that Bishop Tikhon says to Nikolai Stavrogin, "I feel that absolute atheism is more worthy of respect than worldly indifference." When Nikolai replies that Tikhon truly puzzles him, Tikhon clarifies his baffling comment:

> "Whatever you say, a complete atheist still stands on the next-to-the-top rung of the ladder of perfect faith. He may take the last step; and he may not—who knows? But the indifferent, they certainly have no faith, only ugly fear—and only the more sensitive of them have that." (412-3)

Significantly, the good Bishop Tikhon says these words to the evil Nikolai Stavrogin, who represents the *incarnation of indifference*. For Tikhon, the real sin is neither the kind of atheism involved in vital living nor the believers' honest doubts about the existence of God. Rather, the real, fundamental sin is to *negate both life and love*. Indifference is the essence of wickedness because it takes the gift of life and crushes it like a flower in the hand. Evil is self-rejection, rejection of others, and world-rejection. Nikolai is evil because he lacks passion and commitment and because he cares deeply for nothing. He represents the tendency of evil to become a pattern of "nonbeing," a "law of sin," or a fixed pattern of negation. We contend that this law or pattern of evil is what Dostoevsky regards as the demonic. To give way to the demonic is to become walking death, a passionless being who denies personal freedom of choice. In *The Possessed*, Nikolai gives way to random impulses just because he does not really believe in *choosing*. He is possessed of evil just because he is not a person who chooses as

a free creature and accepts the responsibility of his choices. He is possessed because he is dispossessed of the connection between his own acts and the consequences of his acts. He literally dispossesses himself of life and in the end hangs himself with a rope. Ironically, his own Nihilism has strangled the life from him.

Dostoevsky and Karl Barth

Many regard Karl Barth as the twentieth century's most prolific, learned, and influential theologian. Students of Barth and Dostoevsky may be surprised to learn that the two great Christian writers come very close to one another in their distinctive view of the origin of evil. On the problem of evil in particular, Barth the Protestant is not so much a systematic theologian as a profoundly insightful and highly creative thinker. In interpreting Genesis 1:2, Barth rejects the hypothesis that the *tohu wabohu* ("without form and void") refers to an unformed material mass that the Creator fashioned into harmonious cosmos. Barth speaks, rather, of an active and dangerous "boundary" to the creative act itself. The power of God is so great that the *excluded possibilities* to which the Creator said No has a certain reality and retroactive power of its own (74-7, 351).

The question emerges as to how this threatening potentiality exists in relation to the Creator. For Barth, it cannot exist as a self-contained reality outside God, for that would imply a dualism that he rejects. At the same time, Barth does not pull back from postulating an "undeniable risk" which God "took upon Himself when he hazarded creation, but to which, since He is the Creator, He is fully equal and therefore did not have to fear." It is strange to hear a theologian who professes to belong to the Calvinistic tradition speak of "risk" and "hazard" in the act of divine creation. Protestant orthodox theologian G. C. Berkouwer in *The Triumph of Grace in the Theology of Karl Barth* insists that despite this risk and hazard, the "prefiguration of the triumph" appears everywhere in Barth's writings (59).

If the triumph is a foregone conclusion, however, then are the risk and hazard real? Barth insists that the Nothingness (*das Nichtige*) connotes active, destructive power of a wholly negative character. Seeking to improve on Leibniz's philosophy, which had no room for the reality of chaos, Barth does not accept Augustine's conclusion that evil is merely the *absence* of something. For him, chaos always hovers at the edge of all created reality. It can take initiative as a

ruinous, destructive power. Again unlike Leibniz, Barth portrays God as *struggling* against the real threat of chaos. The *triumph* against chaos and evil is real for Barth just because the divine struggle against chaos and the threat of ruin is a real battle and not a pretense. The chaos has being at God's left hand (353).

According to Brightman, the nonrational Given is not created by God but rather touches everything in the finite world just because the nonrational Given is a dimension of God's own uncreated being (*A Philosophy* 337). Barth does not place the chaos or *das Nichtige* inside God. Nor does he contend that it is God's creation. This would seem to leave it, however, in some kind of metaphysical limbo. Brightman does not pull back from making explicit what is elusive and implicit in Barth, namely, that *chaos somehow comes out of God's own being*. Barth, embracing something that in some ways resembles Brightman's doctrine of the nonrational Given, affirms that the divine energy is so powerful that it generates its own conflict and contradiction (74, 351). Even when referring to the threat of chaos as not God's proper work, Barth seems to imply that it is his inadvertent work (349). It is his "opus alienum," the alien and strange work of his left hand, in contrast to his "opus proprium," his proper work (351-3).

Berkouwer, drawing heavily from Volume III, Part 3 of Barth's *Church Dogmatics*, offers the following cogent summary of Barth's position:

> The chaos exists precisely in the fact that it is not God's creature. It is there from the beginning as certainly as from the beginning His Yes implies His No. "Alone with God and His creature, the chaos is there from the beginning. Therefore it has always played a role in the history of God's relationship to his creature." Again, this does not mean a creation of good *and* evil. The chaos is not a creature and still it has reality. (72)

Dostoevsky is certainly closer to Barth and Brightman than to Augustine and Leibniz in recognizing the seriousness of the absurd, the conflicts, and the chaos that permeate creation, especially the human portion of creation. Dostoevsky seems to operate from the presupposition that where there is life, conflict will always appear. His novels reveal with originality and profundity that conscious love itself does not come without conflict and suffering. That is just the way reality is. And apparently, Dostoevsky's God, who is love, is not exempted from the conflict that love knows.

Barth comes close to saying that God in the act of creation could not keep from bringing chaos into existence. In order to cling to his Calvinistic version of omnipotence, however, he is compelled to make a distinction between the Creator's *positive will* and the Creator's *negative will*. While somewhat misleading, this distinction is also exceedingly revealing. Barth appears to be saying that while God did not want all the evil in his creation that we seem to observe, he could not bring maximum good into being without also bringing into being chaos and evil. Did the Creator *want* Auschwitz? Barth does not pose this question for himself, but the answer implicit in Volume III of his *Church Dogmatics* is that evils like Auschwitz are "the inevitable divine negation and rejection," which are the alien work of God's left hand (361). As a Calvinist who wants to go beyond Calvin, Barth insists that *das Nichtige* is only temporary, a "transient necessity" (361), which God has in Christ overcome and which has served his perfect purpose.

Barth contends finally that this is the best of all possible worlds. With unnerving prose, Ivan Karamazov lashes out against this kind of conclusion. The profound similarity between Barth and Dostoevsky is apparent in the unwillingness of either Christian thinker to let the problem of evil lie sleeping. There is an almost frantic desperation in the writings of Dostoevsky and Barth when they deal with the thorns of theodicy. They are unhappy with the tradition that sweeps theodicy under a theological rug. Even when Barth tries to sweep it under a mysterious dogma of divine sovereignty, the lumps under the rug move and become conspicuous.

Like Dostoevsky, Barth admits that he cannot *conceive* of how the world in which human beings live their daily lives can fit into the great "best of all possible worlds." In the end, it is for him a matter of faith, of trust in the Creator's perfection. Brightman and Barth are the two twentieth-century Christian writers most akin to Dostoevsky. Each knew too much about the horror and evil of life to be able to embrace a theology that failed to take evil seriously. If in their desperation they must pound on the door of heaven itself, they will do so. Neither Barth nor Dostoevsky goes as far as Brightman in developing a *systematic* theory of the Creator who suffers original conflict. But all the ingredients of such a theory are in the writings of Barth and Dostoevsky, two of Christianity's greatest rhetoricians. One could almost say that Brightman baked the cake that Barth and Dostoevsky kneaded together but were reluctant to shove into the oven.

Ironically, Dostoevsky's probing and penetrating view of love—as risk, conflict, good will, and forgiveness—makes it impossible for him to silence Ivan's protest against the great "harmony." It is as if there were in heaven itself original conflict that allows for love but will never resolve itself into a perfect, eternal reconciliation. The genie called Ivan simply cannot be coaxed back into the bottle.

Love without End

French philosophers Jean Bodin (1530-1596) and Jean Jacques Rousseau (1712-1778) as well as English philosopher John Locke (1632-1704) and many others have held that human beings need to believe in an after-life of rewards and punishments and in an omniscient Being who reads their inmost thoughts. Otherwise, human beings would lack sufficient motive for behaving (Plamenatz 97). It is noteworthy that Dostoevsky makes no connection between moral behavior and the Creator's putative intimate knowledge of every human thought and wish. It may very well be that Dostoevsky's radical notion of individual free will precludes divine mind reading.

Dostoevsky believes in immortality, and for him it is central to both religious faith and moral commitment. Yet even here he is quite original in the way he deviates from the traditional means of linking immortality with moral behavior. A careful reading of especially *The Brothers Karamazov, Crime and Punishment*, and *The Idiot* discloses that involved and committed love freely given is the axle of Dostoevsky's vision of the moral life. Indeed, in *Notes from Underground*, the anti-hero remains in his "mousehole" primarily because he either does not know how to commit himself in love or chooses to nurture his spite. In Dostoevsky's theology, immortality is crucial because without it love has, he believes, no meaning. And if love loses its meaning because it has been permanently cut off, then freedom, morality, and creativity have no meaning. Death, not life, gets the last word. Immortality, then, is the possibility of continuing the life of freedom, involvement, love, and forgiveness.

The Elder Zosima does not, however, try to make a case for either the existence of God or immortality. Rather, he challenges people to venture to love. "Try to love your neighbors actively and tirelessly. The more you succeed in loving, the more you'll be convinced of the existence of God and the immortality of the soul" (56; bk. 2, ch. 4). The Elder seems to assume that to participate in

love is to share in the Creator's goodness to the extent that one feels or knows that the flow of love cannot truly die. To love is to step into the river of immortality.

Dostoevsky's theology of love and freedom is as subtle as it is profound. He does *not* contend that immortality is required in order to supply human life with something more significant and meaningful than involved love and freedom. Rather, immortality is their full affirmation and extension. *Nothing is required to justify love and freedom or to give them significance*. What they require is the opportunity to flourish in this life and the next. Immortality, then, is the celebration of the paradise of love without end.

The Great Dramatist
and the Created Characters

In exploring Dostoevsky's theology of freedom, looking at the theodicy of a twentieth-century Thomist and briefly comparing it with Dostoevsky's will prove fruitful. In *Philosophical Theology*, James F. Ross advances the model of the Creator as a kind of cosmic dramatist or novelist. The Creator, having written the script for all the players, somehow gives each of them freedom even though no character utters a word or makes a gesture that the Great Dramatist has not prescribed and directed. Despite the fact that Ross seems unable to determine whether the players are actual or are merely characters in the divine mind, his Great Dramatist analogy throws light on Dostoevsky's theodicy.

What Dostoevsky understands and Ross seems not to understand, however, is the *process* of creating characters in a play or novel. Author and character interact so that *each creates something in the other that did not previously exist*. Creation is not a one-way street. Novelists and playwrights readily confess that frequently their characters surprise them and even threaten to take over the story.[1] Novelists and dramatists learn the importance of *listening* to their characters and learning from them so that the writing process can continue. This means that the author of the story does not always carry out his original intent or plan for the story*. The characters have a certain power of their own as cultural creations. Writers have often struggled with their characters because of

---

[1] B. F. Skinner, who has written a novel as well as a few poems, compares "having" a poem to having a baby (Skinner, "Lecture" 345-51).

the characters' unexpected impact on both the author and the other characters of the story.

Dostoevsky's passion for individual uniqueness and freedom was so intense that, according to Mikhail N. Bakhtin, it produced a new kind of literary work, the polyphonic novel. The multiplicity of independent and clear voices and consciences become in Dostoevsky's novels not only objects for the author, but subjects that both talk back indirectly to the author and turn the narrator into another character who must fight for a place in the story. Bakhtin writes:

> In Dostoevsky's works the [single] consciousness is never
> self-sufficient; it always finds itself in an intense relationship
> with another consciousness. The hero's every experience and his
> very thought is internally dialogical, polemically colored and
> filled with opposing forces or, on the other hand, open to
> inspiration from outside itself, but in any case does not simply
> concentrate on its own object; it is accompanied by a constant
> sideward glance at the other person. (26)

Bakhtin's analysis holds more for *The Possessed* and *The Brothers Karamazov* than for *Crime and Punishment*, the first of Dostoevsky's large novels. In reality, throughout his literary career, Dostoevsky never resolved for himself the problem of the novel's point of view because he struggled perpetually with the complicated relationship between the freedom of the characters and the freedom of the author. This complicated relationship of freedom is also, we contend, a *metaphysical* problem that remained central to Dostoevsky's Christian theology. The relationship between the Creator's freedom and the freedom of those conscious and self-conscious creations called human beings proves to be the *supreme* metaphysical problem for Dostoevsky.

In *Dostoyevsky and the Process of Literary Creation*, Jacques Catteau argues that Dostoevsky's detailed plans for a kind of adventure novel entitled "The Life of a Great Sinner" never came to fruition because, in part, they kept feeding into and generating material for other novels. All the great works of Dostoevsky have in some profound way grown out of a single ideal novel that was never written (252-3). To understand this process of literary creation is to understand more profoundly Dostoevsky's metaphysics and theodicy. God the Author produces characters that in turn contribute to the divine-human story or series of

stories. If this author-story analogy provides insight into Dostoevsky's theodicy, then the critical importance of immortality again comes into focus. The divine-human stories continue *without end*, each story having meaning both in itself and in its contribution to subsequent stories.

The Theodicy of Freedom

Nicholas Berdyaev, a Russian writer banished from his own land, points out that freedom lies at the center of Dostoevsky's conception of the world and that his hidden pathos is freedom's pathos. Insisting that Dostoevsky moved him more than had any other philosopher, Berdyaev correctly sees that for Dostoevsky the tragic process of the world is a function of freedom in both God and the human race. "All his novels—his tragedies—are concerned with the experiment of human freedom" so that human destiny lies in freedom, and the destiny of freedom lies in human beings (68). Perhaps Berdyaev's most profound insight into the thought of his fellow Russian writer is that freedom cannot be reduced to goodness or truth. "Any identification or confusion of freedom with goodness and perfection involves a negation of freedom and a strengthening of methods of compulsion.... But free goodness...entails the liberty of evil. That is the tragedy that Dostoevsky saw and studied..." (69-70).

We have offered the thesis that in developing his theodicy, Dostoevsky comes closer to the personalist E. S. Brightman than to any other philosopher of religion because each man takes seriously the risk and open-endedness of freedom. Each sees clearly that tragedy and conflict are at the heart of real freedom. And both seem to grasp that there is ultimate conflict, with freedom always precarious and love never proceeding without risk. Brightman boldly asserts that if freedom is to be taken seriously, then time is real. And if time is real and not an illusion, then the Creator *cannot* know all the future and therefore *cannot* prescribe every event that will come into being. For Brightman as apparently for Dostoevsky, even in the next life the story of freedom and love goes on without perfect harmony appearing on the horizon. Dostoevsky does not come out in the open and say pointedly that perfection in the sense of perfect harmony will never come about in this life or the next. All the ingredients of his theodicy, nevertheless, point to the sober conclusion that perfect harmony is impossible.

Dostoevsky could have embraced the ideal of perfect harmony in the next life only if he had been willing to say that in the next life there is no freedom and

no love. In the last scene of *The Brothers Karamazov*, Alyosha, Kolya, and the other boys gather at the big stone to talk of their young friend Ilyushechka, who has just been buried. Kolya turns to Alyosha and asks if they will rise from the dead, come to life, and see one another again, including Ilyushechka. Alyosha, half laughing, half in ecstasy, replies, "Certainly, we shall rise, certainly we shall see and gladly, joyfully tell one another all that has been" (776; Epilogue, ch. 2). If life and love are to continue in the after-life, Dostoevsky could not strip individuals of the quality that makes them most truly human—conscious freedom. But *where there is freedom, there is always risk and the possibility of both love and evil—even in heaven.* Father Zosima dares to project that in hell itself freedom endures along with the possibility that love will rise from the ashes. This is perhaps why Zosima confesses to having prayed for those in hell who once took their own lives on earth (323; bk. 6, ch. 3).

Dostoevsky is one of the few Christian theologians whose theodicy could coherently account for the possibility of angels "falling from heaven." Ivan Karamazov's critique of the ultimate harmony is haunting and unnerving because he goes for the jugular by questioning the very concept of harmony. If there is freedom, then there will be evil. The price paid for the ultimate harmony is so great that, for Ivan, the price itself cannot fit into the harmony. Dostoevsky the author of the Karamazov story is challenged by his creation Ivan: You must choose between freedom or perfect harmony. Ivan in "The Legend of the Grand Inquisitor" offers his own version of harmony, but the price is nothing less than the loss of freedom.

Chapter XII. Is Everything Permitted?

A Question of Meaning

One of the most frequently referred to passages in Dostoevsky's writings is Ivan Karamazov's statement that if there were no God and immortality, everything would be permitted (263; bk. 5, ch. 5). Jean-Paul Sartre and other writers have made much of this statement, but they have not defined precisely what it means. It is important to nail down the meaning, since Dostoevsky seemed to want to argue that without belief in God and immortality, civilization would

never have come into being (134; bk. 3, ch. 8). An exploration of Dostoevsky's criticism of both the moral philosophy of utilitarianism and the Napoleonic ideal will help us in the search for Ivan's meaning.

Critique of Utilitarianism

Both Charles Dickens and Dostoevsky set out to expose what they regarded as serious flaws in utilitarianism. They believed that this moral philosophy expounded most rigorously by the English philosopher and legal reformer Jeremy Bentham (1748-1832) arrogantly taught that happiness could somehow be calculated and measured. Bentham, spelling out what he called the *hedonistic calculus,* argued that individuals and groups of individuals could use reason to calculate units of pleasure and pain that are suggested by alternative paths of future behavior (Hospers 107-21, 174-98, and 200-26). The utilitarians were accused of advocating the ethic of egoism and of misusing statistics to *average* units of happiness for whole societies, thereby forgetting that individual human beings—not groups—feel pleasure and suffer pain. Dostoevsky in particular insisted that human beings were not the rational animals that utilitarianism and its philosophical cousins supposed them to be. In *Notes from Underground,* his anti-hero actually seeks pain and suffering and scoffs at those who talk of enlightened self-interest.

One of the most ridiculed of the utilitarian ideas was the principle of advancing the greatest amount of happiness for the greatest number of people. It was often incorrectly interpreted to mean that the minority's happiness and well-being could justly be sacrificed in service of the majority's happiness. Instead, Bentham had advocated the principle that every individual counted for one and that the goal of social ethics was that of maximizing the happiness of each individual, thus increasing the general happiness.

Charles Dickens' novel *Hard Times* was written partly as a criticism of what he understood to be utilitarianism. The character named Thomas Gradgrind, who represents the utilitarian in the novel, becomes the butt of Dickens' savage satire.

> Thomas Gradgrind, sir. A man of realities.... Thomas Gradgrind. With a rule and a pair of scales, and the

multiplication table always in his pocket, sir, ready to weigh and measure any parcel of human nature, and tell you exactly what it comes to. (2)

Gradgrind, portrayed as a schoolmaster dedicated to pouring gallons of hard facts into the empty pitchers of his students, refers to one of his students as "Girl number twenty" and scolds her for using her imagination. "You must discard the word Fancy altogether" (3).

While writing *Crime and Punishment,* Dostoevsky, who greatly admired Dickens as a fellow Christian novelist, had perhaps Thomas Gradgrind in mind. In the novel, Sonya becomes a prostitute to save her siblings and mother from slipping deeper into poverty. Raskolnikov says:

> "They say that's just how it ought to be. Every year, they say, a certain percentage has to go...somewhere...to the devil, it must be, so as to freshen up the rest and not to interfere with them. A percentage! Nice little words they have, really; so reassuring, so scientific. A certain percentage, they say, meaning there's nothing to worry about. Now, if it was some other word...well, then maybe it would be more worrisome...and what if Dunechka [the protagonist's only sister] somehow gets into the percentage!... If not that one, then some other?..." (50; pt. 1, ch. 4. The ellipses are Dostoevsky's.)

While Dostoevsky was working on his notebooks in preparation for *Crime and Punishment,* a Russian translation of the book *Principles of Political Economy* by the English utilitarian John Stuart Mill was published in Dostoevsky's city of St. Petersburg. Apparently in response to Mill, Dostoevsky placed the following words in the mouth of one of his characters: "But Mr. Lebezyatnikov, who follows all the new ideas, explained the other day that in our time compassion is even forbidden by science, as is already happening in England, where they have political economy" (14; pt. 1, ch. 2). The debate over the effects and limits of the feeling of compassion on moral behavior has continued into the twentieth century. Behaviorist B. F. Skinner, in an article for the Joseph P. Kennedy, Jr., Foundation for Mental Retardation, argued that since the feeling of compassion is itself a

by-product of contingencies, children and others who require special care need countercontrols in order to prevent mistreatment at the hands of staff members.

> Fortunately, there are those who are inclined to do something about the mistreatment of children, the aged, prisoners, psychotics, and retardates. We say that they *care,* but it is important to make clear that caring is first of all a matter of acting and only secondarily a matter of feeling. ("Compassion" 287)

Far more significant than the debate about the causal power of compassion is Dostoevsky's poignant attack on the doctrine of the principle of the greatest-amount-of-happiness-for-the greatest-number. In a brilliant piece of writing and plotting, Dostoevsky in *Crime and Punishment* tries to show that utilitarianism leads to the justification of murder. According to the story's young protagonist Rodion Raskolnikov, the murdered woman was "a stupid, meaningless, worthless, wicked, sick old crone, no good to anyone and, on the contrary, harmful to everyone..." (65; pt. 1, ch. 6). Why not, then, take her money, put her out of her misery, and use the money to help good people in need? Rodion knows that his sister, whom he loves, is about to marry Luzhin, a small-hearted character, in order to help Rodion out of his financial misery (198; pt. 3, ch. 1). If Rodion Raskolnikov had the wicked old woman's money, he could help his sister, mother, and many others.

> "A hundred, a thousand good deeds and undertakings that could be arranged and set going by the money that old woman has doomed to the monastery! Hundreds, maybe thousands put right; dozens of families saved from destitution, from decay, from ruin, from depravity, from the venereal hospitals—all on her money. Kill her and take her money, so that afterwards with its help you can devote yourself to the service of all mankind and the common cause: what do you think, wouldn't thousands of good deeds make up for one tiny little crime? For one life, thousands of lives saved from decay and corruption. One death for hundreds of lives—it's simple arithmetic! And

what does the life of this stupid, consumptive, and wicked old crone mean in the general balance?" (65; pt.1, ch. 6)

Critique of the Napoleonic Ideal

The genius of *Crime and Punishment* arises partly in the way Dostoevsky attacks both utilitarianism and the Napoleonic ideal of the great man who becomes a law to himself. Bentham's contemporary Georg Hegel of Prussia spoke in *Reason In History* of world-historical individuals like Alexander, Caesar, and Napoleon who grasp the higher laws of the Spirit. "But so mighty a figure must trample down many an innocent flower, crush to pieces many things in its path" (39, 43). Rodion Raskolnikov in *Crime and Punishment* entertains the possibility that he is such a Napoleonic superman, one of the historic individuals who makes rules for others but is himself bound to none save those he uses for his own purposes. To determine if he is truly one of the Napoleonic wonders on earth, however, Raskolnikov must perform an experiment. Unlike Christ, who gave his life, Raskolnikov must prove to himself that he is one of the extraordinary men of power. He must kill the old woman and take her money.

At the very time that *Crime and Punishment* appeared in issues of *Russkii Vestnik* in 1866, Tolstoy's *War and Peace* began to appear in alternate issues of the same magazine. In the history of literary periodicals, none has enjoyed an equal literary feast, with each of the two Russian novels deliberately wrestling with the Napoleonic ideal (Wilson 237). Tolstoy portrayed Napoleon as something of a spoiled, self-centered individual who lacks elementary insight into his own unimportance. A year earlier, March 1865, Napoleon III had published *The History of Julius Caesar* in which he argued that providence produced now and then great men of genius who possessed the duty to cut the path for others to follow. James I of England and Scotland on March 19, 1603, had proclaimed to the English Parliament, "I am the Head, and it [the nation] is my Body." Earlier, in 1598, he had said that the Head might be forced to cut off some rotten members of the body in order to preserve the whole (Garber 100).

In *Crime and Punishment*, the Napoleonic ideal dances in Raskolnikov's head. He believes that if he, like Napoleon, is truly a different breed of man, he must dare to do what all great men of force and power have done even though they were described at the time as criminals. For Raskolnikov, the question is, why

should such a superior person submit himself to the moral laws of ordinary people? Dostoevsky in *Crime and Punishment* produced a psychological novel by tracking in suspenseful detail the process of Raskolnikov's mental states both before and after the murder. It is also a superlative philosophical novel that uses Raskolnikov as an experiment in testing out rival moral philosophies.

The Grand Delusion

In his 1871 novel *The Possessed*, Dostoevsky shifts from attacking utilitarianism, which initially in England had some connection with capitalism, to attacking so-called scientific socialism. Both *Crime and Punishment* and *The Possessed* read as if they had been designed to explore the mind of someone like Lenin or even Stalin. Lenin had read Hegel, who professed to show how the dialectic of Reason and Mind was the true nature of providence. In *The Possessed*, written eight years prior to Stalin's birth, one of Dostoevsky's characters speaks not of the greatest happiness of the greatest number, but of establishing reason in Europe even if millions of heads must roll. It is the general destruction in the name of ultimate good (90; pt. 1, ch. 4). Later in the same novel, Dostoevsky's turns his rapier satire on the utopians who would enslave nine-tenths of humanity—a herd of cattle—for the improvement of the one-tenth. This division of humanity is said to be based on "data gathered from the natural sciences and is very logical" (385; pt. 2, ch. 7). As if this were not a sufficient satire, another character in *The Possessed* proclaims that he would blow the nine-tenths "sky-high, leaving only the well-educated tenth, who would then live happily ever after in accordance with scientific method" (386; pt. 2, ch. 7).

Charles Dickens misunderstood Jeremy Bentham's utilitarianism, and Dostoevsky did not have a firm grasp of either John Stuart Mill's or Bentham's version of utilitarianism. Dostoevsky in particular tended at times to lump Benthamism with socialism of the kind that imagined that a planned economy and social order was possible. Nevertheless, today Dostoevsky's *The Possessed* presents in many ways an on-target critique of the social and economic planners who were prepared to sacrifice millions of individuals for the envisioned utopia. The parody and ridicule that Dostoevsky resorted to cannot, however, measure up to Leonid Brezhnev's laughable speech "The Great October Revolution and Human

Progress," given November 2, 1977.[1] Laughable because of its apparent seriousness, this speech is one of an emperor standing as it were stark naked before an assembly of professed admirers who proved to be either a vast choir of liars or an assembly of self-congratulating victims of their own grand delusions. If today Brezhnev's own words were placed in the mouth of a character in a Russian novel, the author would be accused of using outrageous, heavy-handed satire. The truth is, Brezhnev himself unwittingly gave the most biting and devastating satire of Brezhnev. He spoke glowingly of the "equality, fraternity, and unspeakable unity of the peoples of the Soviet Union" and declared such an achievement as "a fact." It was as if he had stepped out of one of Dostoevsky's novels for the purpose of demonstrating the ludicrous cruelty that human beings can carry out in the name of virtue and the highest ideals.

In *Dostoevsky's Dickens: A Study of Literary Influence*, Loralee MacPike contends that Dostoevsky offers a new lens for seeing Dickens and appreciating him as both artist and social critic (14, 31). Similarly, looking though the lens of the USSR of Lenin, Stalin and the KGB, we view Dostoevsky in a new light and appreciate him more fully as both an apostle of individual freedom and an unsurpassed novelist.

In "The Legend of the Grand Inquisitor," Dostoevsky spells out in some detail a planned utopia organized by an elite core that does not hesitate to perpetrate a lie for public consumption. The lie is justified as necessary for maintaining social cohesion. The literary power of Dostoevsky emerges with a vengeance when his readers come to realize that the Inquisitor's tale is a sword with two edges. Ivan, who relates the tale to Alyosha, leads the Grand Inquisitor, the cardinal himself, down a path that compels him not only to reveal the truth that he and his fellow elitists will deceive their subjects, but to turn on Dostoevsky's Christ and accuse him of being no less an elitist who would sacrifice great masses for the elect few. The Jesuit cardinal, an atheist and elitist, confesses that he regards the masses of mankind as feeble and pitiful children who must be both fed and manipulated. But earlier in the Karamazov story, Alyosha lets slip that his

---

[1]In his capacity as General Secretary of the Central Committee of the Communist Party of the Soviet Union, Brezhnev gave this speech to a joint jubilee session of USSR officials to mark the 60th anniversary of the Great October Socialist Revolution.

beloved Elder Zosima "once said that most people need to be looked after like children, and some like the sick in hospitals" (217; bk. 5, ch. 1).

In accusing Dostoevsky's Christ of being an elitist also, the Inquisitor asks him two penetrating questions:

> "And if in the name of heavenly bread thousands and tens of thousands will follow you, what will become of the millions and tens of thousands of millions of creatures who will not be strong enough to forego earthly bread for the sake of the heavenly? Is it that only the tens of thousands of the great and strong are dear to you, and the remaining millions, numerous as the sands of the sea, weak but loving you, should serve only as material for the great and the strong?" (253; bk. 5, ch. 5)

The Argument of Expediency

Throughout *The Brothers Karamazov* runs the argument that if there were no God, everything would be permissible. This could be interpreted to mean that if there were no Creator, there would be no universe and hence no morality. Starting from scratch, everything would in the abstract be possible and permissible. It is unlikely, however, that Dostoevsky intended to make such a simplistic point. More likely, he means that if the world that we live in exists without God and without realistic hope for life after death, then there is no moral order in the universe and therefore *no reason to love or behave morally*. Morally speaking, if there is no divinely arranged moral order in the universe, then according to Dostoevsky anything goes. Morality is up for grabs. Everything is lawful and permitted because everyone is a law to himself or herself and nothing binds people to one another in love and respect.

The most stinging irony in all Dostoevsky's novels is the one that he perhaps did not himself catch. Dostoevsky stands on the edge of an argument of expediency: even if there were no God and no objective moral order engraved in the universe, people would do well to *believe* that they exist nevertheless. Furthermore, the individual would do well to tell others that God and the objective moral order exist and that life and love will continue after death. In short,

Dostoevsky comes close to imitating the Grand Inquisitor by *recommending the great lie for the sake of meaningfulness and social stability*.

Rejecting The Objective World

There is another irony in Dostoevsky's theology. In *The Brothers Karamazov*, Ivan is counted as wicked for at least theoretically *rejecting the world*. In *Notes from Underground*, however, Dostoevsky uses his anti-hero to reject the idea of *any* order in a universe without God. The anti-hero is a man in revolt against all order. It is as if Dostoevsky means to say that if he cannot have the Christian universe with *moral* order written eternally in the stars, then he will not have the stars. Or at the very least, he wills to deny that there are any lawful patterns to a universe without God. In short, Dostoevsky, using the anti-hero of *Notes from Underground* as his stalking horse, turns out to be a mutineer with a hidden agenda. If he cannot have God, he will not accept the universe as it appears, with its regularities and patterns. Through the spiteful anti-hero, Dostoevsky is saying *No* to any and every universe that lacks God as its source. Dostoevsky the theologian, hovering over his novels, is Ivan Karamazov's mirror image. They are one in rejecting the world, although for different reasons.

It is possible to interpret *Notes from Underground* as Dostoevsky's saying something like the following to his readers:

> All right, so you demand a universe void of God, do you? Well, let me tell you what it will be like to have nothing that is dependable, nothing you can believe or trust except your solitary will, that is, the naked burning light of consciousness. To begin with, there are no laws. Everything is in flux. Yes, everything. So simple a formula as $2 + 2 = 4$ is true only because you *choose* to make it true. But if you choose to make $2 + 2 = 5$, you are "free" to do that also. In the second place, you don't really have a universe *out there*. You have only yourself and your own free choice. You are the Solipsist. That is, nothing exists except you and your experiences. And even your experiences are only what you choose to make them at any

moment. So, you want to be God? Well, have a go at it. Be my guest. Create your own world every morning. Or rather, invent it at every second. After all, your universe hangs only by a thread, and that thread is your personal choice. Needless to say, you can't ask my advice or expect sympathy from me. Not real sympathy, since, after all, I am only your own projection. If you are the Creator, I am only a fleeting voice and patches of sensation in your endless consciousness. If you don't like my advice, dismiss me along with my advice from the universe. Dismiss mathematics. Dismiss love. Dismiss anything and everything that does not suit your momentary whim. And if you don't like your whims, dismiss them, too! But cease all your complaining. If you suffer the toothache, it is your own fault. Did you not invent your own toothache?

Ah, so you like your pain, do you? You, the self-made Solipsist need pain? *Why*, for Heaven's sake? Oops, excuse me. But I don't understand why you need pain. What? To prove that your are alive? That you are real? But to whom will you prove it? The Solipsist has no friends—and, for that matter, no enemies except those of his own mind. But perhaps you need your conjured enemies to prove to yourself that you have a mind—unless, of course, you choose to have no needs at all. All right, I'm leaving. Goodbye until you need me again. But beware of your needs.

Dostoevsky seemed genuinely afraid to admit as a viable possibility the existence of a world containing physical order having no divine source and no prescriptive moral order. Or, perhaps more accurately, he seemed unable to *comprehend* the idea of a universe of physical structure that lacked high moral order. He had *either* to see nature inside the paradigm of theistic personalism, with nature as God's joyous body, *or* to see nature as the cold and cruel enemy having no positive relevance to human love and morality. To his credit, he understood with fierce clarity what some of the Social Darwinists did not—namely, that moral law and human love cannot be *deduced* from the physical laws of nature.

The Evolution of Morality

Dostoevsky's writings do not reveal the extent of his understanding of Darwin's principle of natural selection. While he kept detailed notes on the growth and evolution of his novels, he seems to have had no systematic insight into the way moral rules, principles, and guidelines might have evolved over the centuries, somewhat in the way that languages evolved. His resort to the argument of expediency, ironically, might have set him on a fruitful path for exploring the gradual emergence of morality had he pursued the argument more rigorously. By asking about the *consequences* of not believing in God and immortality, he approached nevertheless the door of consequential ethics.

Dostoevsky's argument that anything and everything is morally possible or permissible in a world without God is somewhat theatrical and subject to misapplication. If nature were the mere projection of the human mind, as some of the more grandiose nineteenth-century Germans imagined, then anything might indeed be possible. Whim would be king or queen. But since nature has a stubborn reality of its own, Ivan is misleading in implying that if there is no God, then human beings can do whatever they wish without enduring the consequences. To be sure, human minds formulate the propositions that they take to be expressive of the patterns or laws of nature; but from that, it does not follow that nature has no patterns independent of human propositions. Nor does it follow that the theories of physicists, astronomers, chemists, and biologists describe the psychological state of scientists rather than a physical world that exists independent of human minds.

Even though moral rules and human ethics cannot be *deduced* from the laws or patterns of nature, they nevertheless could not have emerged without regard to nature's patterns. Regardless of what the spiteful and rebellious anti-hero of *Notes from Underground* may contend, nature provides not only resources, but limitations to human behavior, so that it is plainly misleading to say that everything is possible. Nature, even if not a conscious being, disciplines human mortals when they set out to do whatever they please without paying the price. Nature does not provide ethical rules engraved in stone; nor do the forces of nature operate by a principle of justice. But when human beings seek to relate to one another, their human rules and regulations must reflect some sensitivity to the forces and patterns of nature if the rules are to be of practical service.

Sigmund Freud in a letter to his Protestant minister friend Oskar Pfister suggested that moral rules are like highway codes that regulate traffic (123). Both moral regulations and traffic regulations have emerged within nature and as a part of evolving human cultures. They were not deduced from the laws of nature, but neither did they develop without regard to such realities as the patterned behavior of physical and chemical processes and the gravitational forces.

In 1877 Dostoevsky in the second volume of *The Diary of a Writer* indicated that ninety percent of those welcoming the "new ideas" coming into Russia from Europe embraced the position that if there is *nothing*, that is, if all social and moral ideals are mere prejudices, then "one may do *anything*" (604). In the summer of that same year, he wrote that the progressive ideas, including the very good ones, had been reduced to a formula: "If there is nothing sacred, this means that one may perpetrate any villainy" (761). These two 1877 references can perhaps throw light on the meaning of *Ivan Karamazov's statement that if there is no God, everything is permissible.*

- The first possible interpretation of the 1877 references is that Dostoevsky offers a mere *tautology*: If a person values nothing, he or she will not treat anything as valuable. This suggests that any deed of villainy might be performed against anyone or anything.

- The second interpretation is that *without belief in God, people will not regard anything as sacred.* They will cease to show respect and honor because they value nothing. If a human being is no more sacred than a cockroach, then murdering others will come to be regarded as not morally objectionable.

- According to the third interpretation, even though people may continue to behave morally after losing belief in God, they will have no *reason* or *basis* for doing so. Eventually, they will view their moral behavior as an old habit that they can extinguish when it becomes inconvenient.

Assuming, with good reason, that Dostoevsky held to the second and third interpretations, the fact remains that over the centuries human beings have believed in all kinds of gods and have embraced polytheism in various parts of the world. This fact weakens somewhat the claim of those who would insist that belief in *their* version of God is the only rational basis for behaving morally.

What then can be said about the claim that without belief in *some* God, individuals have no reason for behaving morally? The claim fails to deal with the empirical practicality of moral behavior. Many moral rules and principles evolved and were selected because they helped make the process of living more enjoyable, interesting, and secure. The Elder Zosima states that human beings are created for happiness (55; bk. 3, ch. 4). Evolutionists who are also naturalists do not think a supernatural Consciousness designed them. They agree, however, with those theists who believe that human beings are concerned to gain pleasure and happiness. They agree further that ethical codes and moral guidelines have been selected over the centuries as efforts to render human interaction more peaceful and conducive to the quest for happiness and pleasure. Even Dostoevsky's perverse anti-hero cannot free himself of the pervasive concern with gaining pleasure.

> I reached a point where I felt a secret, unhealthy, base little pleasure in creeping back into my hole after some disgusting night in Petersburg.... Yes, yes, definitely a pleasure! I mean it! And...I derived pleasure precisely from the blinding realization of my degradation (*Notes from Underground* 94)

Dostoevsky's intention, of course, was to try to turn Bentham's hedonistic (pleasure) utilitarianism on itself by calling attention to the fact that some people gain pleasure from despair, an insulting slap in the face, or humiliation (*Notes from Underground* 95). Despite his own intentions, Dostoevsky succeeded in portraying in the anti-hero a dedicated masochist who could not learn from his experiences and who simply lacked the imagination to find sources of pleasure and happiness that did not bring him intense pain and prolonged agony. *Notes from Underground* offers the consistent note that revenge, rudeness, spitefulness, and vindictiveness do *not* contribute greatly to the perpetrator's quest for happiness.

In many ways, Dostoevsky's critique of Bentham's moral philosophy backfired on him in *Notes from Underground.*

Given the species' concern with happiness (which the spiteful anti-hero does not succeed in refuting), certain moral regulations and principles over the centuries and among various clans of the species have emerged to control various kinds of intrusion that create fruitless pain and hardship. In addition, certain ways of encouraging mutual aid and making alliances for common security and enjoyment have surfaced over the centuries. In fact, such alliance-making has biological roots. The human body itself is an intricate interplay of cells forming an alliance for mutual aid. There are advantages in looking at the cultural development of ethical codes, principles, and rules as the expansion of the family circle to include ties and relationships analogous to kinship ties.

Positive mutual aid existed as a part of the family life of the human species' animal ancestors. In a period when certain socialists had entered Russia to argue that family life was a relic to be cast aside, Dostoevsky proved to be one of the most clear-headed and forceful defenders of family life and its value as a nursery for developing both joy and morality. His preoccupation with children in especially *The Brothers Karamazov*, far from being the incidental subplot that some critics have maintained, belongs to the heart of this stunning philosophical novel. Dostoevsky saw clearly that moral education began with the affection, tenderness, gentle correction, guidance, and attention that parents bestow upon their children.

He saw also that the respect, love, forgiveness and duties that make for positive and constructive family life serve as the beginning point for the broader moral life that extends to neighbors and others. Sounding like a late twentieth-century psychologist of child development (Flanagan and Rorty), he challenged Russian parents to give their children positive and beautiful experiences that will serve as nurturing memories for the rest of their lives (*Diary* 762). Denying that children are depraved at heart, he challenged fathers to reeducate themselves and even to ask forgiveness for their past failure to love their children as they should. He went so far as to suggest that nature has placed in parents a tendency to love their own children (*Diary* 770-7).

The beautiful memories of childhood, Dostoevsky contended, prepare the way for the moral life. Very near the end of *The Brothers Karamazov*, Alyosha

addresses the boys whom he has befriended and to whom he is now saying goodbye:

> "You must know that there is nothing higher, or stronger, or sounder, or more useful afterwards in life, than some good memory, especially a memory from childhood, from the parental home. You hear a lot said about education, yet some such beautiful, sacred memory, preserved from childhood, is perhaps the best education." (774; Epilogue, ch. 3)

The Question of the Objective Moral Order

Fyodor Dostoevsky has been called the John the Baptist of modern existentialism. He defends human freedom against the view of human nature as a fixed pattern or essence from which each individual's actions could at least in principle be deduced. Dostoevsky may be compared favorably with the American psychologist and philosopher William James, who advanced the doctrine of relative indeterminism in revolt against what he saw as the "block universe" of theists like Josiah Royce. It is significant that despite his God-filled novels, Dostoevsky nowhere delves with any profundity into the doctrine of divine omniscience and infallible foreknowledge. Dostoevsky's view of freedom, like James', prevents him from openly embracing the view that there exists already a deluxe edition of the universe ready-made, eternally complete, and stored in the heavenly library.

Although Dostoevsky's novels contain seeds of twentieth-century existentialism, they present also the medieval doctrine of the Great Chain of Being. According to this doctrine, a cosmic order exists that can be explicated not only in physical laws but in moral laws. This is not to say that the Newtonians have discovered moral and spiritual laws in nature. Rather, for Dostoevsky, the nature that physicists and astronomers study is an abstraction, which is an extraction from the comprehensive whole of reality. For him, the universe not only is more than Newton's version of nature, but manifests a moral order that preceded the human race.

Unlike many theologians of previous generations, however, Dostoevsky in *The Brothers Karamazov* does not pretend to know the precise points at which the Creator has looped and tied together the threads of the providential fabric. Whereas Dostoevsky might have personally believed that the czar of Russia had by divine providence assumed the throne, *The Brothers Karamazov* seems to resist the temptation to spell out the details of the divine plot. Indeed, the novel works on the assumption that the actors in the Supreme Drama contribute in some mysterious way to the story line and do not speak mere lines written for them from eternity. At most, the novel is compatible with the claim of Hamlet:

> There's a divinity that shapes our ends,
> Rough-hew them how we will. (Shakespeare,
> *Hamlet* V, ii, 10-11)

Hamlet's close friend Horatio does not hesitate to go further to invoke the doctrine of the Great Chain of Being when he states that just prior to the murder of Julius Caesar the graves opened and were emptied, comets streaked across the sky, blood-red dew appeared, and the sun gave forth threatening signs (*Hamlet* I, i, 114-20). This same kind of intimate link between the forces of nature and the human drama appears in Matthew 27:51-3, when Jesus yielded up his spirit, darkness having earlier filled all the earth from the third hour to the sixth:

> And behold the curtain of the temple was torn in two,
> from top to bottom; and the earth shook, and the rocks split; the
> tombs also were opened and many bodies of the saints who had
> fallen asleep were raised, and coming out of the tombs after his
> resurrection they went into the holy city and appeared to many.
> (RSV)

Dostoevsky in his last novel studiously resists the temptation to call on miracles of nature to buttress his theological beliefs. Indeed, he seems committed to the view that all of nature is divine manifestation, and he is uncomfortable with the very concept of miracles as proof of divine providence. When Alyosha's faith is shaken because the Elder's body began to decompose earlier than expected, the

narrator sympathizes with the passionate young hero. He treats Alyosha's expectation of a miracle, however, as an expression of a genuine faith that has as yet neither matured nor seen clearly what it truly longs for, namely, justice (338-40; bk. 7, ch. 2).

Through Ivan Karamazov, Dostoevsky gives voice to the philosophical position that not only rejects the presumption of the Great Chain of Being, but makes human love and nature almost alien realities. Ivan is quoted as having said:

> "[T]here is decidedly nothing in the whole world that would make men love their fellow men; that there exists no law of nature that man should love mankind, and that if there is and has been any love on earth up to now, it has come not from natural law but solely from people's belief in immortality."
> (69; bk. 2, ch. 6)

One of the most eloquent passages in *The Brothers Karamazov* reports Ivan as having said that without belief in God and immortality, not only love but the power to continue living would dry up. Furthermore, without belief in God and immortality, eating members of one's own species would be accepted. Moreover, Ivan believes, people should not only permit the egoism that evolves into evildoing, but also acknowledge it as the most reasonable, natural, and intelligent solution. In short, without belief in God and immortality, virtue should give way to evildoing (69-70; bk. 2 ch. 6).

The Logic of Evildoing

Starting with at least *Notes from Underground*, published fifteen years before his last novel began to appear in print, Dostoevsky systematically set out to show that in a universe without God and for a people without belief in God, morality lacks all foundation and freedom proves to be an illusion. In short, a universe void of God leads logically to immorality and slavery.

The anti-hero of *Notes from Underground* is Dostoevsky's double-barreled attack, first, on the doctrine of determinism and, second, on the idea of freedom without Christian metaphysics. By portraying the anti-hero as a sick and mean individual who breathes resentment and remains incapable of

genuine love and commitment, Dostoevsky set out to expose a life of freedom without God. The anti-hero is a compulsive individual in the grip of impulses, whims, and chance happenings. Dostoevsky's intention in this novella becomes increasingly obvious: to demonstrate in the socially bankrupt anti-hero that absolute chance and necessity are indistinguishable. The anti-hero is a leaf in the wind, blindly driven, without either moral orientation or a meaningful place in a universe that adds up to nothing. The anti-hero's life has no meaningful story because the universe without God has no meaningful story. Self-determination appears as an illusion and a joke in such a world. The anti-hero's definition of freedom seems to be little more than *independence* from all causes, which translates into disconnection from all meaningful attachments and relationships. The anti-hero or Underground Man resists being defined; but so long as he has no definition, he is nothing definite. He bounces around aimlessly, a word in search of a context and meaning. In the end, he loses all capacity for love because he confuses freedom with unfettered caprice.

Like many other Christian apologists, Dostoevsky seemed to think that only Christian believers could truly love—or at least have *reason* to love. For him, disconnected freedom always threatens to turn upon itself, generating a monstrous chaos. Underground Man rejects all definitions of his selfhood and refuses to accept that there is human nature, since to give human beings a nature is to make them alike as members of a species with its fixed traits and qualities. Despite this refusal, however, Underground Man exemplifies that it is the nature of *raw will* to turn social relations into competition for dominance and to become caught up in the circle of hurt-and-be-hurt (Wasiolek 54-5).

As a novelist, Dostoevsky understood the difficulty of presenting in a convincing way the single theological presupposition that only Christian believers could truly love. Such a presupposition might appear naive and even self-serving if it were set forth in novels, particularly in those purporting to capture real human struggle in real life. In many ways, Dostoevsky's novels after *Notes from Underground* represent his attempt to try to make sense out of free will once he has released free will with a vengeance in attacking the scientific socialists and the utilitarians as he understood them. For him, Christian metaphysics and Christian love as exemplified by Sonya, Myshkin, and Alyosha provide the only context for giving freedom direction and orientation.

The Question of Subjectivity

Theologians like Thomas Warren who demand an objective moral code established from eternity fail to recognize that their demand grows out of their *subjective* desire or want. Furthermore, they unwittingly embrace an ethic of consequences when they attempt to show the consequences of having no eternal moral code. Appealing to consequences, however, presupposes that consequences are important to subjective wants and desires. Without wants and desires, moral codes of any kind would be pointless and meaningless. Ivan Karamazov *wants* people to believe in God because he *wants* them to behave morally rather than devour one another in an egoistic orgy.

In *Notes from Underground*, the question of why one should have wants and desires at all does not arise. Their existence is taken for granted, perhaps because to be a human being is to have wants and desires. An individual may desire to extinguish all of his or her other desires, but to satisfy that one desire is, of course, to cease to be a person. In Dostoevsky's subsequent novel, *Crime and Punishment*, the rake Svidrigailov chooses to extinguish all his desires because he is emotionally dead already, having no deep ties to others, no satisfying attachments, no warm and reinforcing memories from childhood, and no profound commitments that give him pleasure or happiness. "The idea of getting involved!" he suddenly thought, with a heavy and spiteful feeling. "What nonsense!" Picking up the revolver, he cocked it and pulled the trigger (509-11; pt. 6, ch. 6).

As a Christian theologian, Dostoevsky demanded an objective moral order that was somehow etched into the cosmos. As a psychologist and novelist, however, he understood perfectly well that morality written in the stars was an abstraction if it did not run deep like a nurturing spring in the human heart as a vital subjective reality. But how does the flowing spring come into existence in each new generation? Dostoevsky the psychologist and novelist understood that it came by transference in childhood. The child who is cared for, who understands that she is cared for, who feels connected and involved, and who feels the bonds of affection and warm commitment—that child will in time learn to care for others and to become committed. Duties and desires become so intricately bound together that the *desire* for goodness can grow strong enough to become a passion and devotion. Indeed, acts of both receiving and giving love may in time contribute so profoundly to emerging personal identity that being a trustworthy

person becomes natural. This is especially true for children who have lived in families where trust is an integral part of the family structure. Alyosha Karamazov's memory of his mother is profoundly important to Alyosha's identity as a caring, good human being.

Ivan, far from denigrating morality, expresses the need for it. But why is it needed? What purpose does it serve? Even though the question goes unasked in the Karamazov story, Ivan moves close to answering it. In the long passage in which he acknowledges that he does "not believe in the [eternal] order of things," he and his younger brother discover that they both agree that love is more than its meaning and that love exists before logic. Although riddled with conceptual confusion, the long passage rings with life in a way worthy of the German poet Schiller. The thirst for life is in Ivan, and he confesses that there are people dear to him, people whom he loves, even though he does not know why he loves them (230; bk. 5, ch. 3).

The confusion in this stunning and brilliant passage comes close to resolving itself. Perhaps it is a mark of Dostoevsky's literary genius that he leaves the reader to struggle with him in gaining insight into the issue of why one should love another person. The answer waiting in the wings is that it is life and not premises that generates love. There is no abstract meaning to which enjoyed life must submit in order to gain justification. What must be justified is any intrusion that would quench it.

At this point, ethics comes into play. Moral order and rules evolve, not as ends in themselves, but in service of the desires and passions of life. Morality itself would be meaningless without desires, love, and passion. The sabbath is made for life and not conversely. Moral order can serve in the traffic of passions, loves, and desires to enhance the enjoyment of life and to prevent the flow of traffic from turning into a degrading traffic snarl.

The Objective and the Subjective

Human morality grew and continues to grow out of human desires. No single desire exists, however, in isolation. The satisfaction of each depends on establishing appropriate relationships with the physical and biological environment. Furthermore, each desire must come to terms with other desires if the organism itself is to thrive or even survive in the intricate reality called nature. Theists who

take seriously the doctrine of *general* revelation believe that the patterns and processes of nature provide resources that human beings can learn to appropriate for satisfying their wants and needs. At this crucial point, theists and naturalists share science, common sense, and moral regulations. They also share the recognition of the necessity of self-discipline in confronting the limitations that nature imposes on the species.

Moral rules, principles, and regulations, far from existing in an antecedent Platonic or Augustinian heaven in a celestial library, have evolved over the centuries, often through trial and error. Students of linguistics have no difficulty in believing that there exists no eternal English or Hebrew grammar in some antecedent cosmic deluxe edition, for they can see how languages have evolved over the centuries. Motorists today can readily understand that the traffic rules and regulations that they daily follow evolved from generations past and are still evolving. Indeed, traffic regulations are moral regulations that have also legal backing.

Using a verbal trick, some people in the ethics debate insist that moral rules have no "objective authority" unless they have existed from eternity. This is comparable to saying that football regulations and rules carry no objective authority for the players because the rules did not exist as an eternal reality antecedent to human history. Freud wrote:

> I cannot honestly see that any difficulties are created by patients' demand for ethical values; ethics are not based on an external world order but on the inescapable exigencies of human cohabitation. (Meng and E. L. Freud 129).

Of course, a measure of world order prior to the emergence of the human species and human social relationships must exist. Much of the universe is so filled with randomness that life and love as we know them could not have emerged in most pockets of the cosmos. On the planet in which the human species evolved, sufficient order occurs to allow for the emergence of human life and morality. Other species have emerged with patterns of behavior so rigidly set that moral rules outside the genetic code and as a cultural innovation proved either unnecessary or comparatively limited.

The human social unit has itself exerted pressure on individuals to support the unit. In turn, the social unit has nurtured individuals and given them reinforcement and strength to master some of their environment. Morality has consequences on both the individual and the structure of the community. The "law" of love that Ivan professes not to observe is the structure and dynamics of intricate social existence along with the rewards that follow. He did not deduce his love for Katerina from an abstract law of nature, but rather *discovered* his love when he refused to take the step that Smerdyakov took toward ultimate moral solipsism. Indeed, Smerdyakov himself knocked on the door of love but failed to enter, preferring instead to yield to his passion for revenge, with the noose fitting around his neck as the consequence of his choice. Revenge was indeed possible for Smerdyakov, but it was *not possible* for him to live the life he chose without embracing also certain ruinous consequences that accompanied it.

Nature does not always affix to each deed the precise consequences that the moral community would prefer to have affixed. If nature should follow the community's preferences, nature might indeed be regarded as a moral order, albeit imperfect. The community often affixes its own consequences, however, just because it cannot count on an amoral nature to carry out sufficient justice or to emit the desired mercy.

Like Shakespeare, Dostoevsky draws his readers into the great universal themes with which every generation must contend in one way or another. Intense philosophical thinkers like Dostoevsky and Shakespeare seem morally compelled to face in particular the question of the meaning of evil and sorrow. Dostoevsky goes even further to probe into the *origin* of evil and the *foundation* of morality. In this book, we have tried to indicate why Dostoevsky's novels perhaps more than those of any other writer have been called novels of *ideas*. Disturbing theological themes and original philosophical ideas appear like powerful weather fronts colliding and exploding inside major and minor characters at war with themselves. In a profound sense, any one of Dostoevsky's novels might have been accurately titled "War and Peace." Every act of will in Ivan, Dmitri, Sonya, or any other major character is an act infused with deeply held convictions and beliefs tested

in the battlefield of the human heart. Every belief turns out to be a willful projection of an embattled person struggling to hold himself or herself together.

Until they read Dostoevsky, some people might never realize how twisted human beings can be or how often an individual will find inside himself or herself the sordid enemy lurking in the shadows. Perhaps the most disturbing and insightful truth in Dostoevsky's satire is that the horrors and evils of life are *human* horrors. Whereas Shakespeare, in attempting to portray disorder, chaos, nothingness, and horror in MacBeth's universe, may call upon the three weird sisters from another world or may have Duncan's horses turn wild in nature and eat each other, Dostoevsky never lets his readers forget that life's chaos, despair, and horror belong to our own human domain. Even the tantalizing exchange between Ivan and the devil is an astounding literary achievement and a work of discipline in which Dostoevsky never allows Ivan to escape responsibility for his devil. In *The Possessed* (or *The Devils*), no supernatural personage enters with any believable force. In the final analysis, the devils are human mortals possessed of wicked ideas, evil plans, perverse intentions, and entangled motives.

Dostoevsky's *The Idiot,* a novel of both tragedy and horror, suggests not so much that demons from another world invade mortals, but that the human heart can turn demonic and generate its own Frankensteins. It is the human heart that is both fair and foul. If for Shakespeare's MacBeth all the world is a stage, for Dostoevsky earth often becomes a wild lunatic asylum in which believing hearts find a paradise of sanity, love, forgiveness, redemptive suffering, and life-affirming passion amid the roaring conflict.

Works Cited

1. Aeschylus. *Eumenides.* Rpt. in *Great Books of the Western World.* Ed. Robert Maynard Hutchins. Vol. 5. Chicago: Encyclopedia Britannica, 1952. 81-91.

2. ———. *Oresteia.* Trans. Robert Fagles. New York: Viking Press, 1975.

3. Augustine. *The City of God.* Rpt. in *Great Books of the Western World.* Ed. Robert Maynard Hutchins. Trans. Marcus Dods. Vol. 18. Chicago: Encyclopedia Britannica, 1952. 129-620.

4. ———. *De correptione et gratia.* Rpt. in *Documents of the Christian Church.* Ed. Henry Bettenson. London: Oxford University Press, 1954. 78-9.

5. Bakhtin, Mikhail. *Problems of Dostoevsky's Poetics.* Trans. R. W. Rosel. New York: Ardis, 1973.

6. Barth, Karl. "Church Dogmatics." *The Doctrine of Creation.* Vol. 3. 3 vols. Trans. G. W. Bromiley and R. J. Erlich. Edinburgh: T. & T. Clark, 1960.

7. Belknap, Robert L. *The Genesis of The Brothers Karamazov:* **The Aesthetics, Ideology, and Psychology of Making a Text.** Evanston: Northwestern University Press, 1990.

8. ——. *The Structure of The Brothers Karamazov.* The Hague: Mouton & Co., 1967.

9. Berdyaev, Nicholas. *Dostoevsky.* Trans. Donald Attwater. Cleveland: The World Publishing Company, 1966.

10. Berkouwer, G. C. *The Triumph of Grace in the Theology of Karl Barth.* Trans. for the Dutch by H. R. Boer. Grand Rapids: Wm. B. Eerdmans Publishing, 1956.

11. Bowne, Borden P. *Studies in Christianity. Boston: Houghton Mifflin, 1909.*

12. Brightman, Edgar Sheffield. *Person and Reality: An Introduction to Metaphysics.* New York: The Ronald Press Company, 1958.

13. ——. *A Philosophy of Religion.* Englewood Cliffs: Prentice-Hall, 1940.

14. Brown, Peter. *Augustine of Hippo.* Berkley: University of California Press, 1967.

15. Campbell, Alexander. *The Evidences of Christianity: A Debate.* St. Louis: Christian Board of Publications.

16.   ——. *Popular Lectures and Addresses.* Nashville: Harbinger Book Club.

17.   Catteau, Jacques. *Dostoyevsky and the Process of Literary Creation.* Trans. Audrey Littlewood. New York: Cambridge University Press, 1989.

18.   Cohen, Jeremy. "Original Sin as the Evil Inclination—A Polemicist's Appreciation of Human Nature." *Harvard Theological Review 73:3-4 (1980): 495-520.*

19.   *Cole, William Graham. Sex in Christianity and Psychoanalysis.* New York: Oxford University Press, 1955.

20.   Conklin, George Newton. *Biblical Criticism and Heresy in Milton.* New York: King's Crown Press, 1949.

21.   Cornford, Francis MacDonald. *Plato's Cosmology: The* Timaeus *of Plato Translated with a Running Commentary.* New York: The Liberal Arts Press, 1957.

22.   Culpepper, R. Alan. *Anatomy of the Fourth Gospel: A Study in Literary Design.* Philadelphia: Philadelphia Fortress Press, 1983.

23.   Dickens, Charles. *Hard Times.* A Norton Critical Edition. Ed. George Ford and Sylvère Monod. New York: W. W. Norton, 1966.

24.   Dostoevsky, Fyodor. *The Brothers Karamazov: A Novel in Four Parts with Epilogue.* Trans. Richard Pevear and Larissa Volokhonsky. San Francisco: North Point Press, 1990. (Both the Vintage and the Everyman's Library editions have the same pagination as the North Point Press edition.)

25.   ——. *Crime and Punishment.* Trans. Richard Pevear and Larissa Volokhonsky. New York: Alfred A. Knopf, 1992.

Works Cited 163

26. ——. *The Diary of a Writer.* Trans. Boris Brasol. 2 vols. [Vol. 1 is Pages 1-560. Vol. 2 is Pages 561-1097.] New York: Charles Scribner's Sons, 1949.

27. ——. *The Idiot.* Trans. Constance Garnett. New York: Modern Library, 1983.

28. ——. *The Notebooks for Crime and Punishment.* Ed. and Trans. Edward Wasiolek. Chicago: The University of Chicago Press, 1967.

29. ——. *The Notebooks for A Raw Youth.* Trans. Victor Terras. Ed. Edward Wasiolek. Chicago: The University of Chicago Press, 1969.

30. ——. *Notes from Underground.* Rpt. in *Dostoevsky: Notes from Underground, White Nights, The Dream of a Ridiculous Man, and Selections from The House of the Dead.* Trans. Andrew R. MacAndrew. New York: New American Library, 1961. 90-203.

31. ——. *The Possessed.* Trans. Andrew R. MacAndrew. New York: New American Library, 1962.

32. ——. "To Apollon Nikolayevitch Maikov." 25 March 1870. Trans. Ethel Colburn Mayne. Letter LV in *Letters of Fyodor Michailovitch Dostoevsky.* New York: Horizon Press, 1961. 190-2.

33. ——. "To His Brother Michael." 1847. Trans. Ethel Colburn Mayne. Letter LV in *Letters of Fyodor Michailovitch Dostoevsky.* New York: Horizon Press, 1961. 190-2.

34. ——. "To His Niece Sofia Alexandrovna." January 1 [13], 1868. Letter XXXIX in *Letters of Fyodor Michailovitch Dostoevsky.* New York: Horizon Press, 1961. 141-4.

35. ——. "To Mme. N. D. Fonvisin." Beginning of March 1854. Trans. Ethel Colburn Mayne. Letter XXII in *Letters of Fyodor Michailovitch Dostoevsky*. New York: Horizon Press, 1961. 69-73.

36. ——. "To Nikolay Niko-layevitch Strachov." 24 March 1870. Trans. Ethel Colburn Mayne. Letter LIV in *Letters of Fyodor Michailovitch Dostoevsky*. New York: Horizon Press, 1961. 186-9.

37. Dowler, Wayne. *Dostoevsky, Grigor'ev, and Native Soil Conservatism*. Toronto: University of Toronto Press, 1982.

38. Driver, John. *Understanding the Atonement for the Mission of the Church*. Scottsdale, Pa.: Herald Press, 1986.

39. Euripides. *Iphigenia in Tauris*. Rpt. in *Great Books of the Western World*. Ed. Robert Maynard Hutchins. Vol. 5. Chicago: Encyclopedia Britannica, 1952. 411-24.

40. Evans, G. R. *Augustine on Evil*. Cambridge: Cambridge University Press, 1991.

41. Flanagan, Owen, and Amelie Oksenberg Rorty, eds. *Identity, Character, and Morality*. Cambridge: MIT Press, 1990.

42. Freud, Sigmund. *Psychoanalyses and Faith: The Letters of Sigmund Freud and Oskar Pfister*. Ed. Heinrich Meng and Ernst - L. Freud. Trans. Eric Mosbacher. New York: Basic Books, 1963.

43. Garber, Marjorie. *Shakespeare's Ghost Writers: Literature as Uncanny Causality*. New York: Methuen, 1987.

44. Gibson, A. Boyce. *The Religion of Dostoevsky*.

Philadelphia: The
Westminster Press, 1973.

45. Gilson, Etienne. *The
Christian Philosophy of
Saint Augustine.*
New York: Random
House, 1960.

46. ———. *Reason and the
Revelation in the Middle
Ages.* New York: Charles
Scribner's Sons, 1938.

47. Goddard, Harold C. *The
Meaning of Shakespeare.*
Chicago: University of
Chicago Press, 1951.

48. Goldstein, David I.
Dostoyevsky and the Jews.
Austin: University of
Texas Press, 1981.

49. Hackel, Sergei. "The
Religious Dimension:
Vision or Evasion?
Zosima's Discourses in
*The Brothers
Karamazov.*" *New Essays
on Dostoyevsky.* Ed.
Malcolm V. Jones and
Garth M. Terry.
Cambridge: Cambridge
University Press, 1983.
139-68.

50. Hasler, August Bernhard.
*How the Pope Became
Infallible: Pius IX and the
Politics of Persuasion.*
Trans. Peter Heinegg.
Garden City: Doubleday &
Company, 1981.

51. Hegel, Georg W. F.
*Reason in History: A
General Introduction to
the Philosophy of History.*
Trans. Robert S. Hartman.

New York: Liberal Arts
Press, 1953.

52. Helms, Randel. *Gospel
Fictions.* Buffalo:
Prometheus Books, 1988.

53. Hesse, Hermann. *In
Sight of Chaos.* Trans.
Stephen Hudson. Zurig:
Verlag Seldwyla, 1923.

54. Holquist, Michael.
Dostoevsky and the Novel.
Princeton: Princeton
University Press, 1977.

55. Homer. *The Iliad.*
Trans. E. V. Rieu. New
York: Penguin Books,
1988.

56. ———. *The Odyssey.* Trans. E. V. Rieu. New York: Penguin Books, 1980.

57. Hospers, John. *Human Conduct: An Introduction to the Problems of Ethics.* New York: Harcourt Brace & World, 1961. This exposition of Bentham's hedonistic utilitarianism is still the most lucid to be published in English.

58. Ivanov, Vyacheslav. *Freedom and the Tragic Life.* Trans. Norman Cameron. London: Harvill Press, 1952.

59. Jackson, Robert Louis. *The Art of Dostoevsky: Deliriums and Nocturnes.* Princeton: Princeton University Press, 1981.

60. Kelly, Aileen. "Dostoevskii and the Divided Conscience." *Slavic Review* 47.2 (1988): 239-60.

61. Kjetsaa, Geir. *Fyodor Dostoyevsky: A Writer's*

Life. Trans. Siri Hustvedt and David McDuff. New York: Fawcett Columbine, 1987.

62. Krag, Erik. *Dostoevsky: The Literary Artist.* New York: Humanities Press, 1976.

63. Krook, Dorothea. *Elements of Tragedy.* New Haven: Yale University Press, 1969.

64. Lehmann, Paul. "The Anti-Pelagian Writings." *A Companion to the Study of St. Augustine.* Ed. Roy W. Battenhouse. New York: Oxford University Press, 1955. 203-34.

65. Luther, Martin. *The Bondage of the Will.* Trans. J. I. Packer and O. R. Johnston. Old Tappan, New Jersey: Fleming H. Revell Company, 1957.

66. MacPike, Loralee. *Dostoevsky's Dickens: A Study of Literary Influence.* Totowa, New

Works Cited

Works Cited

Jersey: Barnes & Noble, 1981.

67. Marty, Martin E. *A Short History of Christianity*. New York: The World Publishing Company, 1971.

68. Milton, John. "The Christian Doctrine." *The Student's Milton*. Ed. Frank Allen Patterson. New York: Appleton-Century Crofts, 1933. 919-1076.

69. Mochulsky, Konstantin. *Dostoevsky: His Life and Work*. Trans. Michael A. Minihan. Princeton: Princeton University Press, 1967.

70. Moore, Stephen D. *Literary Criticism and the Gospels: the Theoretical Challenge*. New Haven: Yale University Press, 1989.

71. Morson, Gary Saul. *The Boundaries of Genre: Dostoevsky's Diary of a Writer and the Traditions of Literary Utopia*.

Austin: University of Texas Press, 1981.

72. Pagels, Elaine. *The Gnostic Gospels*. New York: Vintage Books, 1981.

73. Pareyson, Luigi. "Pointless Suffering in *The Brothers Karamazov*." *Cross Currents* 37.2-3 (1987): 271-86.

74. Passage, Charles E. *Dostoevski the Adapter: A Study in Dostoevski's Use of The Tales of Hoffman*. Chapel Hill, NC: University of North Carolina Press, 1954.

75. Pervo, Richard I. *Profit with Delight: the Literary Genre of the Acts of the Apostles*. Philadelphia: Philadelphia Fortress Press, 1987.

76. Plamenatz, John. *Man and Society: Political and Social Theory*. Vol. 1. New York: McGraw-Hill, 1963.

77. Renan, Ernest. *The Life of Jesus*. Garden City, NY: Doubleday, n.d.

78. Robinson, James M. *The Problem of History in Mark and Other Marcan Studies*. Philadelphia: Fortress Press, 1982.

79. Ross, James F. *Philosophical Theology*. New York: Bobbs-Merrill, 1969.

80. Rousseau, Jean Jacques. "A Discourse on a Subject Proposed by the Academy of Dijon: What is the Origin of Inequality among Men, And Is It Authorized by Natural Law." *The Social Contract and Discourses*. Trans. G. D. H. Cole. New York: E. P. Dutton and Company, 1950. 176-282.

81. Schweitzer, Albert. *The Quest of the Historical Jesus: A Critical Study of Its Progress from Reimarus to Wrede*. 3rd. ed. Trans. W. Montgomery. London: Adam & Charles Black, 1954.

82. Seely, F. F. "Ivan Karamazov." *New Essays on Dostoyevsky*. Ed. Malcolm V. Jones and Garth M. Terry. Cambridge: Cambridge University Press, 1983. 115-36.

83. Shipps, Jan. *Mormonism: The Story of a New Religious Tradition*. Urbana: University of Illinois Press, 1985.

84. Skinner, B. F. "Compassion and Ethics in the Care of the Retardates." *Cumulative Record: A Selection of Papers*. 3rd. ed. New York: Appleton-Century Crofts, 1972.

85. ——. "A Lecture on 'Having' a Poem." *Cumulative Record: A Selection of Papers*. 3rd ed. New York: Appleton-Century-Crofts, 1972.

86. Snaith, Norman H. *The Jews from Cyrus to Herod*. London: The

Religious Education Press, 1949.

87. Strauss, David Friedrich. *The Life of Jesus Critically Examined*. 3rd ed. Trans. George Eliot. Philadelphia: Philadelphia Fortress Press, 1975.

88. Sullivan, Clayton. *Rethinking Realized Eschhatology*. Macon, GA: Mercer University Press, 1988.

89. Talbert, Charles H. *What Is a Gospel? The Genre of the Canonical Gospels*. Philadelphia: Philadelphia Fortress Press, 1977.

90. Tennant, F. R. *The Origin and Propagation of Sin*. Cambridge: Cambridge University Press, 1908.

91. Terras, Victor. "The Art of Fiction as a Theme in *The Brothers Karamazov.*" *Dostoevsky: New Perspectives*. Ed. Robert Louis Jackson. Englewood Cliffs:

Prentice-Hall, 1984. 193-205.

92. ——. *A Karamazov Companion: Commentary on the Genesis, Language, and Style of Dostoevsky's Novel*. Madison: The University of Wisconsin Press, 1981.

93. Tolstoy, Leo. *War and Peace*. Trans. Louise and Aylmer Maude. New York: W. W. Norton & Co, 1966.

94. Walker, Williston. *A History of the Christian Church*. Edinburgh: T. & T. Clark, 1953.

95. Wasiolek, Edward. *Dostoevsky: The Major Fiction*. Cambridge: The M.I.T. Press, 1964.

96. Wells, G. A. *Who Was Jesus? A Critique of the New Testament Record*. La Salle, IL: Open Court, 1989.

97. Williams, Daniel D. "The Significance of St. Augustine Today." *A Companion to the Study*

of St. Augustine. Ed.
Roy W. Battenhouse.
New York: Oxford
University Press, 1955.
3-14.

98.   Wilson, A N. *Tolstoy.*
New York: W. W.
Norton, 1988.

99.   Wolf, William J. *No
Cross, No Crown: A
Study of the Atonement.*
Garden City: Doubleday,
1957.

100.   Zahrnt, Heinz. *The
Historical Jesus.* Trans.
J. S. Bowden. New York:
Harper & Row, 1963.

Index

C

176

F

184

Canonical Biblical References